A LABYRINTH OF LIFETIMES

A LABYRINTH OF LIFETIMES

One soul's journey through many reincarnations….

Kathy Bornino

Copyright © 2020, Kathy Bornino

All rights reserved. Printed in the U.S.A.

No part of this publication may be reproduced or transmitted in any form or by any means, electronic or mechanical, including photocopy, recording or any information storage and retrieval system now known or to be invented, without permission in writing from the publisher, except by a reviewer who wishes to quote brief passages in connection with a review written for inclusion in a magazine, newspaper or broadcast.

Quantity Purchases:
Companies, professional groups, clubs, and other organizations may qualify for special terms when ordering quantities of this title. For information, email info@ebooks2go.net, or call (847) 598-1150 ext. 4141.
www.ebooks2go.net

Published in the United States
by eBooks2go, Inc.
1827 Walden Office Square, Suite 260, Schaumburg, IL 60173

ISBN: 978-1-5457-5277-7

Library of Congress Cataloging in Publication

TABLE OF CONTENTS

Prelude vii

1 Atlantean Herbalist Glimpses 1

2 Roman Sister 4

3 Nun in Piedmont 6

4 Norwegian Woman Loses 2 Babies 8

5 Turkey Shoot 10

6 Man Starving in Prison...14

7 Neptune 16

8 Guiding Bishop 23

9 Mara 29

10 Mara and the Norwegian Courier..................................34

11 Marnie WWI Nurse 39

12 Miriam 43

13 The Large Cat 45

14 Luc 46

15 The Blacksmith 49

A Labyrinth of Lifetimes

16 Woman who deserts her daughter..................54
17 Village leader.....Canadian Hunter 57
18 Black Mama 60
19 Austrian Peasant Revolt Leader..................67
20 Atlantean Herbalist Forgiven......................71
21 Hohn 75
22 Sorcerer's apprentice/victim – Black bird 80
23 Seer in Crete..85
24 Shaman in Polynesia 91
25 Healing the Ancestors – Irish......................96
26 ENUF 103
27 Bellagio Revisited: Monk..........................105
28 A Thread that weaves the stories together ...108
29 Assistants 114
30 Regression Therapies...............................117
31 Importance of Intention............................133
32 Discernment of Dark and Bright Shadow 138
33 Entity Involvement 142
34 Archetypal Energy..................................152

Epilogue..155

PRELUDE

Bellagio, Italy

In my early past life work in Carmel, California, with a therapist trained by Chris Griscolm of the Light Institute in Galileo, New Mexico (featured in Shirley MacLaine's ***Out on a Limb)*** I had received advice from a guide that I should look at pictures and learn to separate out the energy from the form and color, to help me learn to process past life images. So I began the enjoyable pastime of visiting art galleries, which abound in Carmel. I was visiting my favorite gallery with my daughter and was struck by a painting of a village of tall buildings that came down to the water's edge of what I saw as an Alpine village, with a chapel in the distance and high mountains in the background. We went on to view other paintings but over the following months my mind went back repeatedly to that painting and I decided I really wanted it. I contacted the gallery and they suggested I find it in their online catalogue of all past and current paintings. I searched but the painting was not there. The gallery suggested I come up in August when the artist would be doing open house painting and talk with her. I did so. Both artist and gallery suggested a painting that looked somewhat similar, but had modern yachts and low hills. It just wasn't the same. We finally settled on commissioning the artist to paint a version of the painting to be more like I remembered it: no boats, and high mountains. I had quite a bit of dialogue with the artist, Barbara Felisky, who described her great pleasure in going each year to paint in Bellagio, a town on Lake Como. It sounded beautiful and I made a mental note to travel there some day. I received the painting and hung it over my piano to enjoy.

Some years later I was cleaning out old stacks of travel magazines and on the cover of one was Portofino. I saw instantly that was the painting by Felisky that the gallery *did* have. I figured my mind had distorted the painting. I chuckled at its trick. I still wanted to see Bellagio and a few years later the opportunity arose. I was on my own at the end of a cruise and I took a series of trains up to Lake Como. I had booked a reasonably priced hotel room away from the water's edge in Bellagio and took the late afternoon ferry from Como to Bellagio. It was raining as the boat arrived so I hastened to make my way up the hill to Albergo Europa. There was a little field and garden shed near the very plain entrance – oh well, informal, I thought. A lady appeared with my key and told me my room was on the third floor, so I duly trekked up the stairs. The room was plain with high ceilings and French doors which opened onto a courtyard that backed up to a tall building with no rear windows. As I stepped out onto the tiny balcony I could hear chanting – a sweet sound of monks chanting, but I didn't see any windows where the sound could be coming from. I suddenly realized this building complex had not always been a hotel, but must have been a monastery. There were no monks visible now but I most surely had heard them. I chalked it up to simply a vibration in the place. The next morning I explored and sure enough, the Albergo Europa was at the back of a basilica. The painting in the cupola struck me as odd – it seemed like a depiction of a fall of Jesus while carrying his cross but different. The main figure was fully robed though fallen, and a kingly figure was leaning over him with a sword while onlookers jeered. Then I realized that because this was Basilica San Giacomo (James in Italian), this was a depiction of the moment before martyrdom (beheading) of St. James, that same saint who is revered at the legendary resting place of his bones in Compostela, Spain. Sure enough, there were clam shells over some of the doors, indicating this was either a point of origin or stopping point for pilgrims along the Camino de Santiago (James in Spanish). I got chills and then that familiar by now sense of the spirit at work. I walked out into the sunshine and decided to stroll to the water's edge. Bellagio is truly a lovely town with flower boxes in many windows. Lake Como can appear like a wide river. It forms a V and Bellagio is at the inside point of that V. I got to a vantage point and looked across the lake and was dumbstruck: at the far side of this lake that appears like a river was **exactly** the painting I had seen in my mind, which both artist and gallery said she had never painted: the tall narrow colored houses going down to the water's edge, no boats, a chapel further "up river" and the Alps in the background. I knew then I had been here as a monk, and it had been a very sweet life....

I also knew then that a "camino" was calling to me....it was this journey I have made over lifetimes, that I must walk again and write to share with any others that were drawn to it, so their spirits could use any part of it in any way that might be beneficial to them. I chuckled remembering the Brazilian lady I had spoken with on the train to Como, who had worked for years in Italy and was now preparing to walk the Camino to Compostela in Spain...and the American girls and their mother I had overheard in Puy le Dome in France, preparing to walk the Camino to Compostela from the local Cathedral de Notre Dame, on through the south of France and over the Pyrenees...and the friends I knew who had walked the Camino or were planning on doing so....Okay, okay, okay, Spirit... I surrendered to the call, and this book is the result......

Labyrinth of Lives-A soul's pilgrimage

With the popularity of the movie "The Way" has come a renaissance in desire to make the pilgrimage – literally the pilgrimage to Compostela in Spain, but also other treks, some literal to famous archeological places or places of special energy at reputed ley lines, some more symbolic or spiritual, like the pilgrimage into the cultural history of family ancestors.

Perhaps the ultimate pilgrimage is to the Divine center of the Self, the temple within. There are various treks reputed to lead there. Wise opinions differ as to which segments of the journey are necessary and which are detours and deviations.

As GPS technology improves dramatically and we begin to experience something close to driving on auto-pilot, we have also a good metaphor for developing communication with our subconscious. When we form a clear intention, it will help us find the route to our destination. However, like a GPS it can sometimes give us faulty information, and we can also override its directions by changing our mind as to destination and preferred route. We can even leave it sputtering in "recalculating" mode if we make too many sudden changes.

If we meditate regularly or do some other form of spiritual practice that helps us steady ourselves and keep clear intentions, we also develop communication with our spirit or superconsciousness. The combination of good communication with both super and subconscious can facilitate our soul's journey, its pilgrimage to its alpha and omega, its essence and home.

"Those who do not recall history are doomed to repeat it". Whether this is literally true could be debated, but we certainly have an opportunity to avoid future mistakes if we learn from past mistakes. And we know from reflecting on childhood experiences that the past does affect us. We can modify that influence – and gain more control over our response patterns and outlook, and more choice over influencing our future decisions, if we explore our past with the intention of learning from it and improving future outcomes.

This has been my goal in exploring the patterns in my unconscious and seeking to change them. Often that means uncovering and releasing knots of energy where my consciousness and perspective have gotten stuck, sometimes in very uncomfortable places. The release and freedom that result are worth the effort. For me, that has included exploring past lives, to release the complexes carried forward from them, and to gain access to the wisdom and skills locked in treasure troves in those lives.

I also specialize in this work as a therapist, and the overriding principle I have learned is to respect the wisdom of the super conscious and subconscious and learn to follow its lead rather than dictating too much to it. Of course the ego has the right and duty to make decisions – it is the choice point or Chooser. But aligning the ego with the superconscious and subconscious makes for a far smoother journey. It was also famed psychic and western explorer of past lives Edgar Cayce's definition of meditation. My favorite definition of a therapist's role is to follow the client one step ahead – in other words, staying closely connected with the client's current position, yet seeing the potholes directly ahead in order to warn – but not setting the goal or determining the preferred route, although psychological map reading, along with training in tools and equipment, can certainly be offered.

Exploring past lives is not every soul's preferred route or not their chosen route in this lifetime, but for those who may be called to explore this route in some measure, I offer this account partly as a guide for your own exploration, and also an example of the kinds of pathways this route can take, and what can be required to follow it. It has been a deeply rewarding path but not as simple or direct as many people who discover an interest in past lives would like it to be.

The exploration of past lives benefits from various kinds of preparation. A comfort level with experiencing, expressing and processing feelings is very beneficial and usually the psyche will not open the door to memories without this if you are exploring on your own. A trained guide can be a great help with this, even a psychotherapist who does not do past life regression work but regularly encourages emotional expression in therapy can help you accustom yourself to the flow of emotional energy. Body workers who are experienced in facilitating emotional release are another greater resource. Practitioners of myofascial release, bioenergetics, hakomi, Peter Levine trauma release, sensory-emotional release and similar modalities are especially adept at this. A meditation practice is definitely helpful, along with any consciousness raising programs that explore death and dying as normal processes to become more at ease with. All of these preparations send signals to the unconscious that exploring memories is both safe and desired.

What you will find in this book are accounts of a variety of different past life experiences, mostly in sequence as I encountered them in regressions, some recounted in more detail so you can get some of the flavor of actual regression therapy dialogue, as well as an exploration of various past life regression modalities, levels of practitioner training, kinds of experiences that can arise in the course of past life exploration (ex. archetypal energies, ancestor and entity intrusions) and some guidelines and resources for productive past life exploration.

Recovering past life experiences is analogous to walking a labyrinth. You begin at an entry point, you walk in a weave back and forth until you arrive near the center, then back and forth outward again, then return in weaving toward the center again and back outwards again, until you finally arrive at the center. This center can represent the Self at the center of our being. We rest here, then set forth again, weaving our way outward until we arrive again at the entry point. We have a new experience each time we walk the labyrinth, but always we return to the center. This is like the experience of taking on new lifetimes; between lives we rest in the Spirit, Source or Great Self, the Center of our Being – choose your term. This is the ultimate adventure – definitely worthwhile exploring.

I fervently hope that you will benefit yourself now and in your future – and your past! – by exploring your own soul's journey. You will also benefit your descendants and others around you in this and future lives. When famed psychologist Carl Jung was asked if he thought mankind would survive or perish in some cycle of destruction such as world war, he replied: "Mankind will survive if enough people do their inner work."

Godspeed,
Namaste!

ATLANTEAN HERBALIST GLIMPSES

As a young adult and for two decades I was plagued with immune system challenges until I did regression therapy. My senior year in college I dated a Moroccan. We seemed to have known each other forever and were quite close philosophically. He held modernist views of Islam, but there were still radical differences in our upbringing and cultures. I felt the stress of combined attraction and misgiving. At this time I first developed itching responses to grass. Not having a visa to remain in the US, he moved to Paris and I earned a teaching credential. But our relationship did not survive the challenges of distance. From the start of teaching inner city I had a lot of congestion and sneezing.

I met and married an Italian American. He seemed to me to be a crossroads between the Mediterranean cultures that both attracted and scared me, and the safety of familiar American culture. The sneezing and allergies got worse when my first son was born. Allergy tests showed I was severely allergic to many grasses, trees, flowers, molds, pet dander, dust, tobacco and some foods. By the time my second son was born I would sneeze and blow many times every day, with or without any allergy medications. I learned hypnosis to deal with the symptoms, with varying success.

A Labyrinth of Lifetimes

One day I asked myself in a tired sleepy state Why, oh Why did I have such a problem nose? As if in direct response, an image came clearly to me, of a woman in full length dress handing a small flask to a man who had come to her door. I had a sense of puzzlement and misgiving about that image. Another time some weeks after that I saw the same image and intuitively knew the man had come to the woman for healing herbs and she had given him poison....later I realized it was for his wife. This was all I saw of these images for some years, until I traveled to Silver Springs Maryland for my first past life training workshop. Before that workshop I visited the Association for Research and Enlightenment, the Edgar Cayce foundation in Virginia Beach. On the top floor is a meditation room with powerful energy. There I was able to see more images surrounding the man given the flask of poison. I saw that I had been an herbal healer in Atlantis, trained in laws and principles of healing and Light. But I had become envious of this man's wife, who seemed to radiate color and light in her role as teacher and conductor of some ritual. I felt I would radiate light as she did if I had her role. I pushed aside what I knew of karmic law when one day her husband sought my service because she had fallen ill. I saw my chance to make it look like she died of her illness and my herbal remedy was merely ineffective. She left behind a grieving husband and young children. That was all that I saw at that point, feeling guilt and shame, but I knew my allergies were at least partly a karmic retribution from the natural world for the way I had twisted natural remedies against her.

I also sensed that this key incident in Atlantis might have many repercussions. Edgar Cayce said that karma consists of meeting ourselves – meeting and experiencing the results of our actions.

I was to discover lifetimes where I experienced echoes of many aspects of that fatal encounter in future lives – losing a beloved partner to death or separation, the death of my young children, wallowing in grief, burning at the stake when being an herbalist was equated with deviltry, etc. It is not that God punishes: rather, we seek to grow in understanding and heart, and until we can do that intuitively and vicariously, we learn through direct and often painful experience.

ROMAN SISTER

The first past life regression I ever did with professional help was with a hypnotherapist. I felt tension with my Italian mother in law and had made a disastrous (to me) attempt to clear the air. I invited her to share and discuss any issues she might have with me. She took that opening to light into me with all kinds of criticism about the way I kept my house and dressed my three and four year old boys, whom she expected to appear picture perfect at all times. She was vehement about what really were just slight cultural missteps on my part, where I had not known her point of view and assumed she had a positive view of me where I had a positive view of her. I was always gracious but I didn't measure up to what she wanted in a wife for her only son whom she adored. Her reaction seemed to me way out of proportion to the faults she saw in me, really. I felt there might be something else underlying the tension between us.

This was my first visit to a hypnotherapist and I was leery of letting anyone else have control over me – which is not really the case with hypnotherapy, but I did not know that at the time. The first part of the regression unrolled smoothly.

I quickly saw that she had been my younger sister in Roman times. She had been in love with and wished to marry the man who became my husband in that life, an officer in the Roman army. That same man was my husband in this present life (we have since divorced, but were married 37 years). While I was glad for my marriage to the Roman officer, my sister felt unrequited love for him when she did not get to marry him. In our current life time, she has been very fond of her only son. From her point of view he could do no wrong. Her frustration and unconscious resentment explained a lot of her puzzling double messages toward me. But before I could feel at ease with her there were more layers of relationship to uncover and process.

NUN IN PIEDMONT

The scene of the Roman sisters blurred and changed. I found myself sitting at a writing desk in a darkened room. When the therapist asked me what was occurring I hesitated, then responded to her in French. Some form of French seemed to be the language of the woman seated at the desk and for some reason I did not want to translate. I wanted to stay in the experience to see where it went. I watched the woman look around the room and then get up to look down a corridor. From the statues and small murals on the walls, the rooms on either side of the corridor and the hushed quiet of the place, I could tell she was in a convent. She returned to writing some kind of letter but looked uneasy about it. She rang a small bell and a nun appeared, who was sent to fetch a younger nun, who looked to be in her early thirties, with a cheerful face and lively gait. The older nun gave her whatever paper she had written, now sealed with wax, and the younger nun accepted it dutifully, though a shadow crossed her face. I could sense in French the thoughts and feelings of the one who had the role of a mother superior, though I could not understand directly what she said aloud.

The scene shifted again. Time had passed. There was sadness in the convent. Red eyed nuns had been crying softly.

Some misfortune had befallen the younger nun sent on the errand. Apparently such a journey at that time involved hazards. The mother superior seemed cool but tense, almost guilty. She had known the journey was hazardous but sent the younger nun anyway. Why? With a chill I realized she had secretly hoped some misfortune would befall the younger sister, which indeed it had…but now she felt guilty as she took stock of her dark accomplishment. Why had she wished her ill?

With a shock I realized I was myself the mother superior, but this was not a convent where all the nuns had true vocations of service to a beloved Lord. Some women were there because it was a socially dignified place for widows and unmarried women to be. As a widow of means, I came late to this convent and was put in a position of some authority. But in my resentment that my life seemed over, I was jealous of the prettier, younger nun whose embroidery was so quick and dexterous and whose merriment infected all the nuns with joy. After all, though the message needed to be delivered, I was not *required* to do so in person myself, and I was free to send any of the nuns on this errand, I rationalized…..but guilt lingered…..and perhaps lent another dimension to the uneasiness I felt around my mother in law, whom I had recognized as the pretty, merry younger nun whose fingers could fly, with many of the same traits as mother in law, and similar characteristics to my younger sister in Rome.

As I understood better both my own unconscious feelings and those of my mother in law, my relationship with her very slowly began to improve. It would take years before we came to any real peace with one another, but I consider it one of the gains of this lifetime that we seem to have neutralized out the karma between us.

NORWEGIAN WOMAN LOSES 2 BABIES

For years as a young mother I had recurring waking images of a steamy kitchen, sitting by a steamed up window, gazing out but seeing nothing through foggy glass, just sitting, immobilized…. Eventually I began asking repeatedly "What is this about?" One day in a sleepy state of reverie a response to my question arose.

"I see an image of a teenage girl with blond braids, on a farm…. her father is talking with someone….then the farm is gone and I sense the farm girl is the same as the woman in the kitchen, older, but not really as old as she feels…a heaviness hangs in this kitchen, no urge to do anything…the owner of this house is away….he is her husband, but gone often on business, I think on ships. She waits in the kitchen of their home near the port….what is this heaviness, depression…..oh, she has lost a child; there is no reason to get up, no baby crying, no one to take care of, nothing to do, nothing to enjoy….the life is gone out of her…..and always there is steam, from the tea kettle she lets boil on the stove, not a whistling one….she only rouses herself well after all the water has boiled away, absentmindedly refills it and sets it back over the low flame on the stove, which needs more wood, but she can't be bothered, just sitting in stillness, remembering the moment she discovered the second child…yes, SECOND baby, dead in her crib, for unknown reasons…..the doctor was summoned, but could see no visible sign of anything wrong with the child, other than thinness despite her best efforts to provide good milk from the dairy for this baby…..the baby stopped breathing and the mother has barely breathed since then…..At first the husband seemed understanding of her grief, felt the sharp pains himself, but finally he tired of her never moving, and roused himself to go back to sea and leave her to her own morose ruminating….."

I rummaged around this image a few times as it reappeared now and then, but could learn little more from it, except finally a sense of a dark swirling eddy pool….I think she may have drowned herself, but even that was never clear, only the profound grief at loss

And when my own babies were little, I would check to make sure they were still breathing….

TURKEY SHOOT

This was the first regression I did spontaneously on my own. For many years I had found war movies very disturbing and assiduously avoided them. At this time I had two young boys aged 4 and 6. The four year old liked to dress as a cowboy and wanted a toy gun, which made me uncomfortable. One day I was walking through the family room and saw my husband and boys watching a movie. I had no chores pressing at that moment so I sat down to watch also.

We see the story of 2 boys who were runners in Australia. We get to know their competitions, their families and their friendship. Then the scene shifts and we see the boys as runners behind the lines of battle, before field radios were reliable. One boy is shot; the other runs with all the speed he can muster – you sense it is faster than he has ever run in his life, to deliver the message that there is a cease fire, but he does not get there in time, and you see wave after wave of soldiers emerging from the trenches only to be gunned down. This disaster was based on a true story. The movie: *Gallipoli* (scene of a bloodbath between Turks and British Empire forces, over control of the Bosporus Strait at the start of WWI).

After viewing this ending that caught me by surprise I was so unnerved that I confronted my 4 year old with passionate anguish:

"Victor, please promise me you won't grow up to be an army man!"

"Don't worry, Mom", he said solemnly and earnestly…."I'm not going to be an army man…..I just want to *play* with guns…I promise I'm not going to shoot anybody…."

Then I started to think….what if my little boy needed to defend himself as a man…..have I inhibited him so he won't be able to do that? I decided I needed to get a grip on my nightmarish feelings about war.

Soon after this I picked an afternoon when my husband had taken the boys on an outing where I was sure they would be gone at least an hour and a half. I lay on my bed with the firm intention "I WILL to SEE the source of my feelings about war." Soon I began to feel dizzy. I knew I was safe on my bed and could not fall, so I let my feelings sweep over me.

What I first saw was a large plucked bird hanging upside down. A voice inside my head came "It was a turkey shoot".

I saw a frightened blond boy peeping out from under stone stairs where he was well hidden, cringing against the screams and grunts and whoops filling the air. He could hear the dull thuds of axes and see flashes of boots of mighty men who were wreaking havoc and mayhem in his little village. He withdrew even further so not even his eyes were visible until finally there was a silence almost more terrible than screams. He waited hours and then gingerly crept out of his hole, surveying the smashed remains of his village and the bodies of his family and neighbors. Overcome with revulsion and strange feelings he bolted off, not even seeing what direction he was headed in.

A Labyrinth of Lifetimes

After a couple of days of wandering bereft, cold and hungry, he came to a village and the smell of bread drove him directly to the baker. He could mumble only a few words but the baker seemed to understand: news of the attack had spread. He gave the boy bread and took him into his home. The boy became his assistant.

The boy finally began to recover and looked on the baker as his adopted father. He made friends with a few other boys in the village. As he got older he could go on errands for the baker and go off to gather the special wood the baker preferred for his oven.

One day he was returning from a wood gathering outing when he noticed there was no sound coming from the village. It was strangely quiet – too quiet. He entered the village gate carefully, and then saw it – the same scene of blood spattered everywhere, dead bodies with faces frozen in pain or terror, smoke rising that was not from chimneys. And there, lying face down in a pool of blood still oozing from a giant gash in his back, his beloved baker.

It was all too much, too painfully familiar. He ran off in shock, wandering the countryside, not caring where he was, cold through the night, too much in shock and grief to think any more about survival. He wandered in a confused, dazed state until he died of exposure.

It seemed to me his spirit was still dazed, frozen in shock and terror and grief. My heart went out to him. The budding therapist in me reached out, calling to his spirit, assuring him he did not have to wander alone in the cold anymore. I told him he could come eat and warm himself in my home and he would never have to feel abandoned and alone any more. With that I could feel a rush of tears well up inside me, and I cried deeply, pouring out the grief and fear and loneliness that seemed to have been his.

Eventually I felt calm and relaxed and I knew the boy would be all right. I did not understand completely what had happened, but I knew I had experienced some kind of release. Confirmation of the value of that release came the next day. I was at Mass and prayers were requested for the victims of a massacre of a village in Guatemala. I prayed for them, with peace in my heart. That surprised me, because I knew that up until then such a story and request would have been very troubling to hear, making prayer difficult, but now my heart felt very much at ease.

(See my book, *Armchair Travel to Heal the Planet*, for suggestions on how to switch from a distressed response to gruesome news to a healing response that can help victims.)

MAN STARVING IN PRISON
(BRIAN WEISS REGRESSION WORKSHOP)

Before I ever went for extensive individual past life regression work I attended a seminar workshop with pioneer psychiatrist Brian Weiss (*Many Lives, Many Masters* and *Through Time Into Healing*, along with other later books). He recounted his groundbreaking work with a patient whom he treated with standard hypnosis and suggested she return to the root experience that had triggered her symptoms, expecting her to connect with some childhood trauma. Instead, she recounted a lifetime in ancient Egypt. This was the beginning of Weiss' practical experience that many psychological problems have their roots in previous lifetimes, and clearing the problem is facilitated by returning to that experience and understanding at a conscious and cellular level that it belongs to that other lifetime, rather than staying stuck in the illusion that the trauma is happening at this present moment, which is how the brain sometimes stores traumatic memory, and consequently perceives current experiences through that distorted filter. I very much liked Brian Weiss, who has an almost unbelievably gentle energy. Being around him brings to me the image of taking a bath in warm milk.

Kathy Bornino

I was intrigued and looking forward to the experience of regression in a group. I was an on-and-off meditator, had learned self hypnosis to manage asthma and allergies and generally had little difficulty with most guided imagery experiences. I settled into the quiet in the darkened room.

It seemed to me I saw nothing but dark, which was puzzling….. all too soon Brian Weiss was gently talking us up out of the experience, and I was vaguely disappointed to have seen nothing but dark, until right at the end I saw a dark shape scuttling along a side wall of rock, and I felt a chill…and I knew the place I had been was a dungeon where it was indeed dark, and rats large and small were my company. My stomach wrenched as I realized in a flash I was a relatively young man in his prime slowly starving to death in a kind of prison, where eventually the rats would gnaw on me without further resistance…

Needless to say this gross imagery left a lot to resolve….the pieces of this lifetime came to me slowly over years…..but I will leave the continuation of it as it occurred sequentially, with other individual and workshop regressions and trainings intervening before I was able to return to this lifetime, other than a recurring image that seemed to me to belong to the same lifetime. I would see a country road or long carriage lane, with trees along one side that I seemed to know were poplar trees, and a feeling of great nostalgia as I passed along this road, perhaps riding a chestnut horse…..and one other image or feeling that seemed connected to that lane of poplars was my fondness for warm brown old furniture with gold tones and some inlaid woods, which I would notice in antique stores or people's homes and think "that's not it but that resembles it"……I had only these fragments for many years….

NEPTUNE

When I first felt I needed help with Past Life Regressions (as distinct from the two I had done on my own) I chanced (!) to read Shirley MacLaine's <u>*Dancing on a Limb*</u>. She recounts sessions with Chris Griscolm of the Galileo Institute in New Mexico. I liked the acupressure approach Griscolm used since I still had hesitation about putting myself under the influence of a hypnotherapist. Her protocol induced regressions by acupressure, pressing the "windows to the sky" points near the juncture of the skull and the neck. I decided to make the great effort to go to the Galileo Institute (great effort due to the expense and the chronic difficulty of finding childcare that would fit my family dynamics.) The Galileo protocol stipulated four sessions over four days, plus travel time from the central coast of California to New Mexico which would have involved 2 days each way – 8 days total. When I called to book the sessions I was advised to intuitively pick a practitioner from the list of names and phone numbers provided. However one of the phone numbers had a different area code – 408. That number was in Santa Cruz, an easy 3 hour drive up the coast from my home, to Carmel. A boon from the universe! I would not have to spend extra money and days away from my husband and children. When the timing is right and you are aligned with soul purpose, the universe often clears the way before you. I selected that 408 phone number and made the trek.

The protocol required four 2-3 hour sessions on consecutive days. The first session was supposed to focus on early childhood trauma. I didn't have any major childhood traumas other than a few psychic experiences that scared me and I did not know how to handle. I had already done personal therapy in the process of obtaining my license as a psychotherapist, so we proceeded to the required session of contact with the Higher Self. I hoped this would work but wasn't confident, because my previous attempts to contact my Higher Self or a guide had gotten repeatedly stuck at the image of a bishop with a staff, which alarmed me and I could not seem to get past that, no matter what affirmation process or relaxation methods or alternative suggestions I tried. This time I was guided to form the intention of meeting my Higher Self and just let unfold whatever would come to me.

That was my goal, so imagine my surprise when I found myself swimming underwater which at first was enchanting. I have felt drawn to the water since I was little, despite swallowing mouthfuls of water during my early swim lessons. I began to feel out of breath and felt a little panic and thought I should head immediately for the surface, but I sensed there were dolphins nearby. I kept swimming anyway, fascinated by the enchantment of the underwater world. Some dolphins came by which excited me and I began to realize I could either breathe or manage ok without breathing so I enjoyed the seaweeds and the coral. Next I heard a loud, intense, booming sound that seemed angry. I felt alarmed. Then I heard a muffled sound which quickly grew louder and louder, sounding angry.

I was afraid the voice was angry at me: perhaps I had intruded in this realm. The intense, booming sound continued. I felt the voice reaching out to reassure me that this anger was not directed at me. As the booming got closer it resolved into distinct words.

"You ….CAN… NOT…. MAKE…. ANYTHING…. UP!!! THAT IS MY DOMAINE!!!".

"You — CAN—NOT—MAKE—ANY—THING—UP!!! YOU CANNOT CREATE ANYTHING…."

I realized with a start that it was the voice of NEPTUNE. Neptune was not angry *at* me: he was angry *for* me.

By powerfully laying claim to his own domain as creator of images, he himself was addressing a doubt that lay harbored deep within me, ever since my mother's well-meaning answer to many images that scared me as a young girl. When I would tell her I was afraid of shadows and dark figures in my room, she would tell me either that I had too much imagination or that I should stop making things up. "Stop making things up….go back to bed". Of course, that answer had never helped, only added a new layer of anxiety and guilt: now I was not only frightened of images I saw, I was bad and guilty for seeing them, which did nothing to make them go away. It only added to my fear and compounded the seeming power of fleeting images, as well as trapping me in silence, which plays havoc with a child or adult's imaginal world. The only other thing my mother could think to help me with scary images was to limit my television watching to bland kid shows when she saw that many shows could be alarming to me. Now Neptune himself was stepping in as a powerful divine authority, putting things back in proper order to reassure me.

Kathy Bornino

As an adult and an astrologer, I knew that Neptune was the god of the sea and the imagination and the astral plane, the dominion of which latter plane he shares with his daughter Aphrodite (Roman Venus), goddess of desire. I felt deeply relieved and comforted by this voice once I understood Neptune was making a declaration about the law of imagery; he felt to me like a kindly and protective Grandfather, to whom I felt an instant bond of affection. I never really knew my grandfathers. My mother's father died of TB when she was 9 and I only remember my father's father napping in his chair. (Napping can be a portal into the dream world which is also governed by Neptune, but that is another story.) I was very happy to realize this powerful benevolent protector had been watching over me since I was little and probably before that. I don't think Neptune is my Higher Self but he was certainly the best person/force for me to encounter at that point. I had always loved to swim, especially in the sea. As a teenager I spent many happy afternoons diving under waves in Malibu. But I had never felt a direct connection with Neptune. Of course I knew that Neptune, Poseiden in Greek, was the mythical god of the sea, but I would never have imagined him as a representation of my higher self. Now he felt real, larger than life, calming an old storm in my psyche, which had kept me from feeling safe in the world or with God.

Neptune went on to explain some principles of imagery to me. "You cannot make anything up. That is my domain as creator. You can only choose which images to watch, like channels on a television. Images come to show you something, and you choose what to see." Then he told me how to reduce my fear of scary images.

"An image is just a picture with energy in it. Spend time looking at pleasant pictures and seeing the energy in them. Then practice seeing them without the energy in them, or with different energy in them. What makes images scary or sad or angry is the energy you put into them, or the energy somebody else put into them. You don't create the image, but you can put energy into it, or drain energy out of it. You can send the energy into safe directions. Practice with comfortable pictures first, until you can feel what you are doing. Then little by little, you can practice seeing more energy-filled pictures, and separate the images from the energy, and redirect the energy."

He told me the reason I was so alarmed by images when I was little and periodically since then was because some images were connected with memories of events that had elicited strong feelings, because the events either happened to me or happened to someone else whose experience I tuned in to. Feelings were just energies, he said, and he advised me to try to separate the pictures from the energies attached to them, and then dissipate the energy by realizing I was safe and the emotional energy could either be expressed in some way or just allowed to dissipate on its own once it was separated from the picture. This made sense but he knew that I was still easily disturbed so he suggested I practice doing this with safe, even beautiful pictures. He told me I always had the power to choose which channel to watch on my inner mind screen. He had given me keys to disarming what could seem like time bomb memories.

Neptune had metamorphosed into a kindly grandfather, giving me the answer to a perplexing dilemma that had plagued me for as long as I could remember: what to do with scary images. Since I was doing these past life sessions in Carmel, I began going to art galleries to study the paintings and sculptures, separating the images from the energy in them, unlocking a wealth of feelings which might be the artist's or might be the viewer's, sensing the energies in the colors. Images began to lose their power to terrify me (more correctly, *my* power, as I came to see).

Thus began my prime motivation for visiting art galleries whenever I get the opportunity: to practice separating and joining and separating again the pictures and sculptures from the feelings and sensations they evoke. At first the energies seem to BELONG to the painting or sculpture which can feel overwhelming, but it IS possible to separate them. Long afterward I realized Neptune had given me instructions on how to break down psychological complexes, by finding the impression evoked by an original event, which gets stored as some kind of sensory memory – visual, auditory, kinesthetic physical sensation, smell or taste – as well as an emotional response and a thought, often distorted or focused on a narrow slice of a situation. This thought tries to sum up the experience and lays the groundwork for a belief, which has a tendency to program subsequent similar events. Dealing with the components separately is sometimes a safer, easier way to deal with them, all the time remembering that we are HERE, NOW and safe in this present time frame.

I have studied art ever since, not really for the artistry or the history or the technical composition, but to understand the nature of energies within images. This prepared me to delve deeply into past life regressions, which were filled with disturbing images and memories. I learned that memories are just pictures with energy in them that wants to be released, preferably in safe therapeutic ways rather than re-enacting the dramas we repeat from one lifetime to another.

This was a key assurance for me, that enabled me the next day to finally grapple with the blockage that had kept me from encountering my Higher Self, that image of the bishop.

GUIDING BISHOP

Encouraged and more secure with the assistance of my Grandfatherly Neptune, I was ready to try again to contact my Higher Self or Inner Guide.

In my early days of guided imagery and trying to contact an inner guide, very often I would get stuck at the image of a bishop with miter and crosier (staff). I would feel a vague dread and my mind would jump around to other topics. The day after I encountered Neptune, the bishop came to life for me with startling depth. Up came the sense of roadblock again, but this time I was able to stay with the image instead of fleeing from it, and that opened a portal into a troubling event in which I was a woman watching a procession go by, a hood on my head, trying to be unnoticed in the crowd. In the procession were some men tied together with their heads bowed or turned away, trying as best they could to fend off the fruit and miscellaneous bits being thrown at them. My heart wrenched when I saw that one of the men was the man I loved deeply. I did not understand why he was in trouble but I knew it had to do with things he said that the church authorities objected to. I could not understand the ideas but what I knew for a clear certainty was that he was a GOOD MAN. He was kind to everyone and I loved him deeply, and he loved me.

Then I saw him – the Bishop, the same one I had seen in my attempts to pierce the veil and contact my Higher Self or Guide. How confusing – surely this could not be my Guide!!

I could see him moving past me in a procession and could feel the cloak I was wearing to help conceal my presence by blending in with the crowd. I felt confusion and foreboding. The Bishop saw me also, when my gaze went to him. I looked away but I had seen a glance of recognition in his eyes. After that I kept my eyes lowered as the gruesome procession continued, to an open square where scaffolds had been erected. The prisoners were declared heretics who had not repented and they were each tied to a post jutting up from a platform on which wood and kindling had been heaped. The fires were lit and the smoke and odors emitted made my lungs burn and my stomach retch. My heart contracted into a tiny hard ball in my chest.......

Later I found myself in the bishop's office. He was trying to persuade me to denounce a man I thought was good – a man I loved, in fact, and whose goodness I was absolutely sure of. I could not understand why the bishop insisted that some differences in words and views between himself and this man I loved meant that the man was bad because he would not change what he said. It made my head swim. The one thing I knew for sure was that the man I loved was a truly, deeply completely *good* man.

Not long afterward, several of us were brought to the center of town. Scaffolds had been built, with brush for fires around them. They were going to burn us! Earlier my beloved had refused the bishop's demand, and was tied to a post to be burned. One by one, the others refused the demand also, except for one fellow who had only recently sat in on talks around a circle with my beloved. When it came my turn, I could only think of how awful and empty the world was without my beloved. I made up my mind to be with him wherever he had gone. In all my confusion, he was the only thing that was clear for me. Still, panic gripped me when I found myself before the Bishop and was told I must speak out and condemn the man I had loved and watched die…..I could not understand any reason why…..I only knew he was a GOOD MAN, and the words against him would not come….. I had felt my life go out of me when I watched the man I loved, this GOOD MAN, collapse into the flames.

The words against him would not come so before long I too mounted the scaffold and smelled the fire and the smoke choking me…. I could not breathe…. I was scared as the brush began to burn. There was a lot of smoke. I began to cough in the smoke, trying to shut it out by closing my eyes and not breathing. Smoke searing my throat and chest is the last thing I remember of that life, except for a cloud of confusion all around me….and I knew no more.

That explained to me why I sometimes had seen myself psychically wandering in a grey cloud. Something of that cloud of confusion stayed with me; I recognized it as a haunting image in this life, though it often seemed more like fog than smoke, or maybe the smoke image blurred with fog from somewhere else. What I do know is that any smoke I would inhale, even inadvertently, would set off bronchial spasms that could easily lead to coughing fits. I love to camp, but I didn't dare sit by a campfire. I had to stand, always ready to move away from the direction of the smoke, which always seemed to seek me out wherever I stood. Before restaurants became non-smoking,

I would have a lot of throat and chest tension throughout a meal if anyone was actively smoking, even if I was in the non-smoking section.

But as I reviewed this life, I realized that an inner smoke was even more troubling: because the bishop was our religious authority, it was deeply disconcerting to me that he would have me or the man I loved burned at the stake. I knew the man was a *good* and godly man, and I did not understand how I had done anything wrong by loving him. I could not believe otherwise. So was I not to believe all the priests and bishop had taught? This confusion created a crisis in faith for me that plagued me in this life as well, though I was very spiritually oriented and still loved the symbols and central Christian mystery – which after all had a man of complete goodness at the center of it, who was also executed.

And how could this bishop be a guide figure for me?! No wonder I had never been able to get past the confusing anxiety I felt when I would see him, nor could I settle into any fruitful imagery process leading to a guide prior to this regression.

There should be a "post mortem" to any regression experience…. time spent in what Tibetans call the Bardo state, an altered state of consciousness in which there is clarity, intuition flows easily, guidance can be called in, a person can meet again those they have lost or injured or been injured by…

In this case, I could see and finally hear clearly the Bishop, expressing his regret to me, explaining that he thought he was doing the best for the immortal souls of both my lover and myself, and only later had he come to understand the damages he did to both of us. He thought he was doing what was good for my soul, what would save me from error that would have damned me. When he saw the confusion that resulted in me, he took on the task of helping me work through that confusion. He would stay by me, helping to ward off other energies that would have caused me further confusion, and patiently providing me with a reassuring presence, even though his presence also generated fear in me due to the memory associated with him. This message resonated deeply with me and led to a profound cathartic release, after which I could clearly feel his presence and the image of him no longer inspired dread or flight into distractions. He stayed with me for a few years afterward, helping me sort through how to participate honestly and comfortably in religious rituals and still maintain independent thinking and a clear heart.

Part of his reparation was to become a guide for me in this lifetime, to help me meet the right people that would help me sort out confusions about the Church and its teachings that would arise for me in this lifetime and that he had stayed by my side to bless and protect me, despite unknowing fears of him that would rise within me from time to time. I could finally understand why he would appear to me both as a guide and as a threatening figure, could forgive him his errors and accept his good will, and realize many fortunate encounters in my life that he may have helped facilitate. For example, I had intuitively known the truth of reincarnation since reading the Upanishads when I was 12 evoked a powerful feeling of recognition in me. But what to do with this as a good practicing Catholic, apart from rattling a nun with questions in theology class in high school? An answer came so "serendipitously" (Jung coined this term for an uncanny meaningful coincidence) when I was teaching high school English. I taught a class on term paper writing.

One of my students did good research to present a paper which introduced me to Edgar Cayce, whose work became my inspiration for reconciling traditional Christianity with reincarnation. I could feel gratitude well up in me as I realized the long and patient service of my guiding Bishop, who understood the confusion and doubt his actions had caused my soul, and labored so long to correct and relieve my distrust of spiritual assistance and leadership. As I reflect on this today, I think that Bishop may be a major reason why I am still a practicing Catholic while most of my metaphysical friends who were raised Catholic have long since left the Church for Buddhist or Hindu teachers or Unity or Church of Religious Science or other groups, native American or women's circles or no spiritual community at all.

After this regression I took a bath in water with plenty of bicarbonate of soda to clear my energy field and etheric body as well as relaxing away stress in my physical body. Energy cleansing after any intense regression is a recommended practice to clear away residues which sometimes linger.

MARA

Many people do not know the power of fantasy, to become addictive, to deceive you, to sap your energy, to draw unwanted energies and beings into your life. Nor do they know how archetypal forces or other beings can insidiously enmesh themselves into a fantasy. I certainly did not know the danger when I was 13 and began to entertain what I thought was a harmless fantasy of a teen age singing idol who became entangled with a woman who was a clandestine freedom fighter. In my fantasy he was pressured to entrap her by agents of a powerful foreign government who made threats against his brother's family because that government wanted to cripple the woman's effectiveness and that of her entire resistance organization. An odd fantasy as I think about it now. I certainly had a crush on that singing idol, but the fantasy never became sexual at all, even though he fell in love with the woman he was supposed to sabotage and tried to figure out how to avoid betraying her while still protecting his brother's family, even while he functioned as a double agent pretending to help her freedom fighter resistance forces. The freedom fighter's name was Mara.

The fantasy began when the singing idol's TV show was dropped – as a way to enjoy thinking about him, to engage

A Labyrinth of Lifetimes

him in a story where I could watch him. But nothing in public knowledge of his life was remotely like my fantasy, other than the fact he did have an older brother with a family. The fantasy began to take on a life of its own and it was fascinating to see what would happen. There was a repeating theme of betrayal of trust and the woman agent being fiercely determined and successful at revealing nothing when she was captured by the agents of the repressive government (generic communist – this was the early 60's). Mara was beautiful, highly intelligent, athletic, could master other languages and could easily fit into any situation – a sort of master spy super heroine. She had endurance and unshakeable will, despite repeated capture and torture. The identity of her friends and co-conspirators was safe no matter what was done to her. She would devise ways to go inside her own mind and be mute no matter what was done to her.

A couple of years into this recurring fantasy I gradually became aware that I was no longer choosing to have this fantasy – it would come unbidden and fill my waking thoughts, even when I should have been paying attention to math or history or homework or whatever the subject at hand. By the time I turned sixteen I was frightened by the power of this fantasy to take over my thoughts, and it became increasingly negative and violent. There seemed to be nobody I could talk with about this strange occurrence; I didn't want anyone to think I was weird or simply tell me to stop making things up. I felt that if I were simply making things up I would have been able to stop, but I was quite obsessed or addicted by that point. I found myself particularly drawn to Norway and to stories of the French Resistance in World War ll. I certainly was not bored in school at that time: I carried a heavy college prep load, was on the debate team, played piano and varsity tennis and participated in choir and drama productions at school. But I began to have the very uncomfortable feeling that someone else was with me and wanting me to keep activating this fantasy, someone foreign to me and frightening. Almost instinctively I knew I had to devise a strategy for having no free time to think, no time when the fantasy could steal into my thoughts.

My English teacher suggested I had the talent to do an independent study project and if I produced a substantial research paper she would see about possibly getting me course credit from a local private college. I seized on the opportunity. I was also in a book discussion club with an English teacher from a different local high school where we had just read Hemingway's *A Farewell to Arms*, so I decided to do a research project on understanding the mindset of the writers of the post World War I Lost Generation, and how their world views showed in the characters they created. I delved into Hemingway, Fitzgerald, Dos Passos, T.S. Elliot, Gertrude Stein, and others. Working my project as well as keeping up with all my other commitments meant I was sleeping less than four hours many nights, but at least I was so tired when my head hit the pillow that I could confine the increasingly demanding presence to only a few minutes of my mind before I dropped off to sleep from sheer exhaustion. By doing this I gradually recovered control over my thoughts, or at least kept out the disturbing fantasy and presence. But I had the uncomfortable feeling they were not far away, in a shadow waiting for me to make a mistake or let them back in. The lack of sleep took a toll and by summer I had a barking bronchial cough. My beloved older brother who could drive took me and some family friends to the beach at least twice a week and in the sun and surf and diving under the waves I began to feel cleansed and regain some confidence but there was still a sense of something Other not far away. At that time I was not familiar with auras.

I would still get a wave of anxiety if I thought I had made a mistake, especially in human interaction or someone might be displeased with me, and I would still wake up at times in a panic. The VietNam war was raging and despite avoiding television and news accounts I was plagued with war scenes that would come to mind unbidden. I went to Catholic school and senior year we had a retreat. The priest was an intuitive who had us draw and share the colors of our feelings about ourselves. What I remember vividly was the individual encounter with him, which we were each invited to. I told him I was not interested in going to confession because I felt I had lost my faith, but what troubled me were images of war even though I did not watch television and rarely read the news. He looked at me a long moment and then declared "You are at war with yourself. There are two of you". The moment he said that I felt a loud bang in my head and suddenly found myself on the floor sobbing beyond any words. He read a little passage out of a book of reflections and waited for the storm to pass. I thought I might never stop crying but eventually the tears subsided. I still had no words and no understanding but something radical had happened. I felt a mighty weight lifted off me, I could breathe deeply and I was aware of brilliant color all around me and realized I had been seeing the world around me in shades of grey for months, who knows how long. Though I still felt a deep flush of embarrassment I could talk to select people again and tell them of my feelings, which I had not been able to do for much of my high school years.

Except for occasional recurrences of my nightmare, the sense of a foreign presence seemed to be gone for many years until one night a close friend/ high school teaching colleague and I used a Ouija board. It was her board and she was used to using it with her sister who was not there that night. They had never had any negative experiences. I was curious about my strange high school experience and asked the board who Mara was. The answer came back "an evil spirit". I felt a cold fear creep over me and we stopped using the board and decided it was time for bed. I was to sleep downstairs on a sofa bed. But as I got ready I felt a paralysis of fear coming on and I was terrified I would return to the condition of not being able to talk or move so I literally crawled up the stairs fighting off the sense of paralysis all the way, until I got to the light of my friend's room and felt safe sleeping in her sister's bed. In future I would read voraciously to find answers but not try to confront my experience so directly!

When I first heard Roger Woolger's tapes on Past Life Regression I felt a connection to him, and when I watched his video I knew I had to work with him. That meant having to fly to the east coast at a time when finances were tight and no insurance covered past life therapy but my desire to understand and relieve chronic anxiety meant I enrolled in his week long workshops several times.

MARA AND THE NORWEGIAN COURIER

One of the most powerful and life changing regression therapy sessions I had was a private session with Roger Woolger, the master regression therapist under whom I later did extensive training.

As I arrived for my appointment with Roger Woolger, whom I knew only from his video of his work, I was sweating and felt faint, not normal for me. We went right to his regression therapy room, which has a mattress on the floor so the body can be free to move. Roger sits beside the mattress to guide as needed. But in my case the story could hardly wait to pour out.

"I have a recurring image and sometimes wake up with a disturbing dream I can't remember but it feels related to the image or some variation of it……It is night time and I am walking quickly toward a bridge over a river in a city….there is a fence as well as a railing on the bridge….but when I get to about the middle of the bridge, a light suddenly shines on me from behind and there is another light aimed toward me on the other end of the bridge. I try to see if I can scramble over the fence and jump into the water but shouts are commanding me to STOP……I am very afraid and wake up or push away the image."

"Ah… your memories are just under the surface….just let the story come out…"

I thrash around on the mattress "They are taking me somewhere…"

"Where are you now?"

"In some kind of office with a single light bulb….a man is waving an envelope at me…..it looks like an envelope I just delivered to a house nearby….I had a bad feeling when I delivered it but it was my mission so I did it….Now this uniformed man is shouting and waving it at me….he wants me to tell him more about it….I don't know much but I am afraid he will make me tell him something……." More thrashing around…."he hits my face with the back of his hand and my head jerks sharply to the left…"

I am quiet and still. "What is happening now?"

"I think I'm dead….I don't think he meant to kill me, just scare me….but my neck snapped"

(a flood of intuitive knowing)

"I was so afraid of revealing anything to this Nazi bully that I left my body and gave it to a walk-in" (a walk-in is a being who takes over a body by consent, and agrees to finish its life mission as well as adding any of its own agenda that it can manage the body and brain to do) In this case, "I gave the body to a primitive being I knew would not be able to operate my memory bank to reveal anybody's name to this interrogator…. she only got to use the body for a few hours and then had to let it go because she couldn't revive it…….but she has stayed with me because I did invite her in at that moment, and haven't ever been able to get rid of her since then…..she is the one who plagued me through my high school years…..I am afraid of her…"

"Would you be ok with my talking with her?" Roger asks.

I nod.

"Tell me your story," he suggests gently.

A different voice emerges that doesn't feel like my own. "We have been walking and walking, for a long time" she rasps. "We cannot find water"…..

"Who is 'we'?" Roger asks.

"All my group…(of families)"

"And what is your name?"

"Mara"

"Do you know what is making it hard to find water?"

"Every time we come to a water hole, it is bad water…… because we have been cursed?"

"Why were you cursed?"

"Because we drank water from a watering hole that was not ours…..and the owner had us cursed, to search always for water without finding any good water to drink…and so we search…..we have been searching for a long time….."

"Would you like to be free of this curse?"

"Yes…" but she has never heard of this possibility, and she is taken aback.

"And if you get free of this curse, will you leave Kathy alone?"

She nods, "but what about the others?"

"You can be free of this curse…..you can all be free of this curse…..if you refuse to accept the curse any longer…."

"But what about the man who cursed us?"

"He doesn't really have the power to make that happen unless you believe he has that power and you accept the curse….your leaders and all of you can dissolve this curse by refusing to accept it anymore, and then you can go find good water to drink…"

A light of realization comes to Mara and the others with her. They find themselves at a pool of good water. The room is brightening. I feel her energy dissipating and leaving me.

I am exhausted, drained, but I feel peaceful and more calm than I have felt for a long time. "Wow! I thought she was evil, and she has been hanging around for so many years, even though I would push her away and think I had succeeded in getting rid of her…." I breathe for a few minutes.

"Let's go back to the woman who gets caught and interrogated…..let's see if you can take back possession of her, and find peace for her?"

"Yes, she is relieved to be dead and not have revealed anything…. she was so afraid of that, which is why she called out for any kind of help available and let in an entity……..and now I see they already knew something before I delivered that letter… they were already waiting for me, and I sense they would have taken me whether I delivered it or not….all my life I have lived in dread of making a mistake, especially with a paper…. every once in a while out of the blue I sweat filling out or turning in a paper, and then I tell myself that's silly, but now I know why, and I DIDN'T MAKE A MISTAKE, or cause my capture and death by delivering that letter, BECAUSE THEY ALREADY KNEW!!!"

This regression provided huge relief that has stayed with me. I sometimes still feel a tiny flurry of alarm as I am about to put a letter in the mailbox, but nothing like I used to feel. Now I am able to feel the difference between an echo from the past that I easily breathe away, and a warning from my intuition that there could be a problem with the letter or form currently in my hand. That clear warning system I feel sure has saved me on a few occasions, from sending a message or feelings to someone that I would later have come to regret. This is an example of both the freedom that regression therapy can bring AND the honing of an intuitive gift that arises out of traumatic experience.

MARNIE WWI NURSE

When I arrived at my first Roger Woolger training in Silver Springs Maryland my assigned roommate was a girl from Colorado who came from an air force family. She felt a strong urge to be the subject of the first demonstration, since she had recently had again a recurring nightmare. She would wake up in a cold sweat among engine sounds. From recalling this dream she entered the regression very quickly, and found herself piloting a bomber over Germany in WWII. She was haunted by the scream of falling bombs even though she could not have heard them from her altitude, and haunted by the screams of civilians below, especially children. Following Roger's protocol, the pilot continued the regression through to later events in that lifetime, including struggling with memories when he came back to civilian life stateside after the war was over. His death occurred when he drove his car around a bend where it hit a slick spot and careened into a ditch. He was badly injured and could not extricate himself from the car. In the intuitive "bardo" state following the regression, he felt relieved that it was an accident that released him from this life, rather than a suicide, even though in his dying moments he also felt a pang to be leaving life behind.

In debriefing this regression it emerged that my roommate's uncle had returned traumatized from WWII and died in a car wreck shortly after. The family never knew whether he might have committed suicide. Roger pointed out two possibilities here: first, that this regression was truly my roommate's former life, or second, that this was a case where a family was plagued by a trauma and the psyche of an unquiet spirit of a family member senses the possibility of relief or assistance through a sensitive family member, in this case my roommate. It seemed probable that the uncle was both traumatized by his war experiences and wanting his family to know he had kept his honor and not committed suicide. Not infrequently, one or more family members will be disturbed by or even live out a repetition of other family members' traumas or belief systems, spoken or unconscious, but clear upon reflection on behaviors and attitudes. Later we would explore this more in family ancestor healing workshops.

What this session triggered for me was that I also could hear the screams of those on the ground. That night I awoke with a splitting headache, like a bad migraine but I had never had such a headache at night. Previously I had only gotten migraines in response to too much sun or wind or cold or heat or bright light. This was different. I calculated whether I could make it to the bathroom before I would throw up, which was my body's usual response to a migraine. But then I realized I hadn't eaten for several hours, there was nothing in my stomach and I didn't actually feel nauseous; I just had a headache which felt like my head was literally splitting apart. I flashed back to a time I was visiting Chinese New Year in San Francisco, in the evening when the streets were full and Asian boys of all ages were everywhere, setting off firecrackers in all directions.

Kathy Bornino

I have always had a strong startle reaction and HATE hearing balloons pop. I looked for my friend in the crowd and a safe avenue to head toward but saw neither and….that was the last I remembered until I found myself lying on a bench outside the Mark Hopkins Hotel, high above Chinatown. I had a vague recollection of being carried. My other friend who I had not seen all day had noticed a tall man carrying me up the street from Chinatown. My friend recognized me and joined the man carrying me. He told her he had seen me faint and decided I should not be in that crowd scene. He decided I would be safe at the Mark, and left me in the care of my friend. This was February 4, 1968 and he was an ex-soldier who had done a tour in VietNam.

It occurred to me as I lay in bed in the middle of the night after the first evening of the regression training week that I could be experiencing some kind of regression spontaneously, since I had had previous spontaneous regressions. I decided this was a safe place to explore that. I tried to relax and suddenly knew that my head had indeed literally exploded from the shock wave from a bomb blast which scattered my body parts in many directions. As I digested this the intensity of pain in my head began to ease off and I got a sense of having been very close to an exploding shell….it came to me that I was a nurse, not usually this close to the front but I had been dropping off some kind of medical supply where it was needed…the name Chateau Thierry came to me, which I knew was a WW I battle site. My name came to me…Marnie, and my age 29. I had volunteered as a nurse after a relationship that didn't work out, for unclear reasons. I had thought to be of service as a volunteer but I had not planned on losing my life, and I was profoundly sad not to have a future returning to England….

Since this was my first workshop and there was so much to learn, I did not realize the importance of working through the emotional content in a regression to release emotional energy stored with it, and when I came back to California I found myself deeply sad on and off for a few weeks, not my normal emotional state at all. I realized but Marnie was grieving not having a life and another opportunity for love….she was despondent and a little bitter that her life seemed to amount to so little….I finally talked with her and told her she would have other chances at life and love, and her pain seemed to fade gradually from my awareness after I did that.

Years later I visited the graveyards of crosses at Chateau Thierry….a very moving place, tranquil in the lush French countryside in 2000, with both death and life in the air….but there were no graves with women's names on them. But then, there would have been nothing of Marnie to bury….

One thing that gave this regression validity for me was that I could henceforth watch fireworks at 4th of July comfortably lying on the grass not far from the fenced off launching area. I love the colorful patterns in the night sky so before this regression I used to lie on the grass telling myself I was safe despite waves of discomfort. I still don't like the suddenness of popping balloons, but I no longer feel any wave of panic in response to them.

MIRIAM

The following regression arose very quickly in a breakout session in regression training where we paired off to work with partners. I needed no guidance on this one but was again glad we always did this work lying down, because I think I would have fallen down or collapsed from the intensity of the feelings it brought forth.

"I see him across the courtyard. Many people are crowding around him but I catch a glimpse of him. My heart beats faster. I can think of nothing but him. There is something so strong about him, yet so gentle. ...Such stories they tell about him..... they say he cures people......I feel better just being this close to him....."

"I lead a very simple life in my village..... (long pause, then sobbing)"

"What is happening now?" (from my guide partner)

"My friend has told me that the great Rabbi is dead...... my chest hurts so much, I cannot stand the thought that he is no more.......My heart is breaking....(much of the rest of this regression is aching in the chest area, and cramping that curls me forward around my chest)............Peace....I have died........I can see him again, in the distance......in blazing light, ahh....I still have a profound sense of sadness, grief and longing.....but at the same time a deeply satisfying knowing that he still IS.....and I will see him again one day....."

THE LARGE CAT

I am a young woman, really a teenager, dressed in leather skins. I belong with a small group of people. We are on the move, using temporary shelters in a ring around a main fire. It is late afternoon and I go to gather roots or berries or whatever other food I can find. Suddenly I feel I am being watched and I grab my basket and run toward the camp, but it is too late. I feel a searing pain in my left shoulder and I stumble and fall from the impact of some large furred animal. I feel its claws rake down my back and legs. I scream but it is over quickly.

I was able to let go of this lifetime fairly easily, maybe because the attack was so quick and final that I had no time for reflection or regrets. In my current life I am allergic to pet dander, especially cats. I wondered whether that might come from this attack, but a psychic later told me out of the blue that I have allergies to animals because I have an affinity to them and I would spend a lot of time with them if I didn't have this allergy, and my soul has other priorities for my time and energy in this life.

LUC

Our induction to this regression was to move to music with our eyes closed, just feeling our bodies, sensing energy in various parts of our bodies, and letting our awareness be drawn to a place in our body where we feel a tension that we recognize has been there for some time, that feels like it has a chronic aspect or is "old".

My attention was drawn to my right hip area, a dull ache that was usually only perceptible if I paid attention to it, but I recalled sometimes feeling a noticeable twinge there. Was that an old strain from overuse from carrying my babies on my hip sometimes? Had I thrown something out of alignment? The conscious mind is ready with explanations that may have a grain of truth in them, but the unconscious often has a deeper story.

As I settled down onto the mat and let my hip sensation lead me into deeper experience, I felt myself to be a tallish, lanky, somewhat awkward man. I am lying down, aching in pain all over my body but especially in my hip.

"Where has this pain come from?"

Immediately the pain intensifies as I feel my elbows and shoulders pulled in one direction, my feet and legs in the opposite direction. I gasp for breath – it feels like even my breath is being pulled out of me. I realize I am experiencing the wooden horror called the rack.

My name is Luc and I recognize my language is an old form of French. I have no idea why this torture is happening to me. I am a simple peasant who used to have a strong body. This horror seems to have something to do with my belonging to the lord of the chateau, who has enemies. I have never been able to understand much about anything.

My body is all broken now, and I die. But things are even worse after I die. For some reason I do not know, they will not bury my body in the churchyard, where I would be protected. I am very uneasy…. I need the prayers said over me…

"See helpers come to your body, Luc….they could be animals or angels or elves or anyone who comes to your need….who comes?"

"I see foxes and bunnies….here they are like friends and work together…..they are building burrows and a den around me……they will keep me company……and they bring a monk who says the prayers over me…….so important to have the prayers……now I can sleep in peace."

Notes: Having the monk come to say prayers over the dead body is an example of completion work done in the "bardo" state of altered consciousness. Without these completions, souls can hang on to uneasiness indefinitely. In this case, I also saw a chiropractor for some body work after this regression. His exam revealed that my right leg is in fact longer than the left, and the x-ray showed evidence of what he described as intermittent slippage of the ball out of the socket in my right hip. Wearing a compression belt and doing some hip repositioning treatment along with making sure to sit on firm though cushioned support relieved the problem of the hip ache.

Note 2. I recently have had problems with my left hip threatening to give way under me. The chiropractor I visited recently told me that I still have the right leg longer than the left, and should wear a little lift under my left heel. This has been a valuable help and is even gradually reducing a bunion on the left foot. This is one more example of completion work- in this case bodywork and realignment -that we don't realize still needs to be done after a past life regression brings us information. It is also an example of how the deeper reason for a body condition may never come to light because we assume that body misalignments are simple anomalies or that they must have developed from causes in this lifetime.

THE BLACKSMITH

When I came back from my first training with Roger Woolger, I was pulling my wheeled suitcase behind me, heavy with bargain books I had bought at the Association for Research and Enlightenment book sale in Virginia Beach. And then I helped my son remove a patch of cactus from our landscape, which involved some heavy shoveling. Perhaps that combination was one reason (but not the only one) why I developed a frozen shoulder, which was extremely painful. The family practice doctor took one look, did nothing and referred me to an orthopedist. I was many weeks waiting for an appointment and waking up at night in tears. When I finally saw him I told him I needed my shoulder to be in shape to travel because I was determined to go to the east coast for another regression training week. He worked with my shoulder under anesthetic to break up any calcium or other deposits, sent me to physical therapy and I got myself to the next Woolger past life workshop.

The first topic discussed was the prevalence of physical ailments that had plagued participants, and Roger explained that the body often will scream a symptom or precipitate an accident or injury in order to get our attention to understand and resolve a past trauma. That was in the background when I did my first trade off session with Mark, who came to be a powerful healer for me, as I also was for him at times in exchange sessions.

The pain in my shoulder and upper arm was still very much in my awareness and Mark asked me to move carefully into the position where the discomfort was strongest…

"What are you aware of?"

"My arm is tied to a pole…"

"Where are you….what is going on?"

"I'm tied to wood coming off the mast of a boat….there's others like me also…we are captives snatched in a raid and I don't know where we are being taken…..but my arm hurts terribly now…

"Move forward in time to the place where you are released from the pole….what is going on now?"

"We have landed at a small port, really not much more than a large village, and each of us is being taken by somebody….. I seem to be given to a black haired man with dirty smudges all over his clothes and his skin…he takes me with him to a simple wooden house near a fire pit and iron works…he is a blacksmith….I understand that I have been given to him….. he is repulsively dirty, but doesn't seem mean, almost shy…but when I make a move to leave the house he blocks the door….he is obviously very strong and makes it clear I am not to leave the house, so I back down…in a little while he takes the rope off my arm and offers me some bread and some kind of drink…. this is a very cold place I have come to, with snow all around, and we were several days at sea, always lashed to the pole…I am exhausted and fall asleep…."

"What happens when you wake up?"

"I think of Cedric and I am so sad….I am afraid I will never see him again…."

"He is my fiancé, a fair haired and beautiful man I love dearly, but he was not there when the raiders came, so he was not killed like other men in our village, praise be to God….but I doubt he will ever be able to come so far to find me….he has no boat and when raiders from the north come our people just do what we can to hide and survive…..the raiders are so fierce and well armed….our men never go after them…."

"Move forward and see what of importance happens next…."

"The sooty black haired man leaves me alone with some food and water for a few days…..and then…..ugh, yuck, gross…..he takes me to bed with him and makes me his woman…..I feel so gross and dirty…..I feel like my life is over……." (Mark is also a body worker, and he helps me wrestle with repugnance of sex with this dark, dirty man ……..we do this for a while to release some of my revulsion)

"Move forward now and see what develops in your life…"

"I live always with the blacksmith…he was stolen from a southerly territory years before. The blacksmith doesn't speak the language of these people, only a little….he was also captured in a raid and brought here, but when they discovered he has skill as a blacksmith they treated him well enough and he made many fine swords for these hated raiders. … they are pleased

A Labyrinth of Lifetimes

with his work in iron….he can make things their blacksmith cannot…..that's why they gave me to him as a wife…..a few times he gives me some piece of jewelry, a brooch to fasten my cloak… He offered me a crudely made bracelet as a gesture of valuing me, but I would not wear a token of affection from a man who was not Cedric."

I have 3 children for him… who bring me pleasure and consolation when they are young. My boys grow up wanting to be members of this village clan, even though they are not….. but as they grow up they prefer to speak the language of the Norsemen and they grow apart from me. There are times when I feel sorry for the blacksmith, because he is an outsider here as I am, but then he is so disgustingly dirty from the soot, and I can never really get clean here, the soot is everywhere, seeps into everything….I am cold to him….the smoke makes me cough…my boys are growing into young men now, and turn their backs on me….they refuse to speak my language that I taught them….they want to belong here…..I am sad and alone…..I cough more and more often……

"What else happens that is important, or how does this end?"

"The cold and the soot and the loneliness have worn me down….I am tired and it is hard to breathe…..I am so very tired and alone….. I never stop grieving Cedric and somehow want to be loyal to him. I can barely remember Cedric but maybe if I pass from this life I will see him….so hard to breathe that I lay down one day and don't get up….I am gone…."

"Now that you have passed through death and can look back at this life, is there anything about it that reminds you of your current life?"

"My shoulder, which has a dull ache but doesn't hurt so much now....and my HUSBAND!!! (I realize with a shock) ... the blacksmith I was enslaved with in that Nordic life is my husband in this current life....and now I regret that I was so cold to him,....we were both victims and he was trying to make the best of the situation while I....I could never get over my grief at losing Cedric, but really the blacksmith tried in his own way to be gentle and kind to me, but I could never feel warm toward him... I died bitter, without ever learning to appreciate my husband's efforts to make my life more tolerable. No wonder I feel a shudder when he walks in the door...and he has the same black hair and beard and dark brown eyes...."

I returned home from this regression determined to be a warmer, more appreciative wife – even when my husband's clothes and his fingernails are dirty!! In the blacksmith I recognized my husband of this lifetime who is also dark haired, but only grimy when he works on cars. At the time of the regression he was a master mechanic doing engine conversions on Jaguars and other foreign sports cars. This regression helped me understand a curious pattern that had developed with my husband, which had grown increasingly pronounced and troubling over the previous several months. All day I would miss him and look forward to seeing him, only to find myself feeling annoyed and repulsed when he walked in the door at night – for no reason I could fathom. Now I could understand that. AND he was my Roman husband who chased the Christians out of our house and forbid me to associate with them......But in this life, after all, he hasn't DONE anything wrong!! Thankfully, after this regression, that curious repugnance faded away.

And, though I am still cautious with it, the frozen shoulder doesn't bother me anymore.

WOMAN WHO DESERTS HER DAUGHTER

At a time of challenge in my relationship with my 18 year old daughter I experienced this regression:

"I live in a mountainous, rocky place…well above a river. Life is crude, simple, hard. I am a woman. I wear loose fitting clothes but not all the way to the ground so we don't trip. I have sandals of a sort. There is never really enough food but we get by…..there is little flat land for growing grains…the women hunt for berries and wild onions and there are a few nut and fruit trees on the slopes….the men fish the river and hunt for rabbits and very occasionally manage to kill a deer, but there are not many of them…. My man has been gone for some years now. He was a hard man, but we had more to eat when he was here."

"My joy is my daughter…but she is almost of marrying age now. There is a man who wants her but I do not like the looks of him…he raises hackles on my back. He is not a young man…..She has no dowry…and no father…he will have his way with her, and it is done …She belongs to him now….."

"He is a cruel man…he beats her whenever he is angry…that a fish got away, or he missed a kill, or the rocks are hard on his feet, or she doesn't please him, or any other thing that bothers him… they live nearby….it tears at my heart to hear her cry out…"

"Now she has a little one, a girl…birth is never easy but Fortune smiled…...he does not seem glad or proud of the baby…. instead seems to resent the baby, and my daughter is forced to shield the baby from his anger….in anguish I go sit above the river, on a ledge where there is a natural rock shield at my back….I am so angry at him I don't know what to do…. the river gives me some comfort….the sound of the rushing water over the rocks is soothing….but then I go back to my little lean-to, built out from a boulder with a shear face, and I hear her again, and the wails of the baby…my heart is torn and I am soooo angry!!!"

"When he is not around I go to help her and comfort her as best I can…she gives me a little meat that she hopes he will not miss…..he does not like me….she is glad to see me and have me hold the baby while we look for berries and wild peas…. but at her house she is always tense, dreading the moment he appears at the door but hoping he will bring back food."

"Many moons pass…and now my daughter has a baby boy as well as her daughter. The man seemed pleased to have a son…but now he is more foul tempered than ever. I see my granddaughter cower, and my blood boils. I go often to the river now and gaze down at its roiling waters, dashing and crashing on the boulders below….it cools me a little….I need solace more than food….but when I return to my little place that is falling down I am so sad when I am not angry….I feel so frustrated and powerless….he does not like it when I go there so I never go if he is there….he knows she gives me a little food….my daughter tries not to cry out when he beats her, but I hear him, and I hear my granddaughter screaming…..I wish he were dead, but they would likely starve without him…there are so few other people along this river…and any good hunter would want his own children, not another man's blood…"

"I go to the river in desperation….I am so angry…he has beaten her again….the river looks angry, which suits me….it seems the river is angry along with me….we are angry together….it seems to me we belong together….the river understands me….the river calls to me….draws me to it, demanding me to join it….I feel so hopeless….I can't save my daughter….I am so angry that the river is my only comfort, and it is calling me to join it….the waters look cool and soothing and inviting….I feel such a strong pull….I can't stand it anymore…..I leap in….I break bones on the rocks and I panic …but then the cold water is numbing…and soothing…. and there is comfort here in the river….the river seems like some grandfather who really does understand and pulls me down into his embrace….I let go…into his long watery arms….."

In the bardo I go as a spirit to visit my daughter….

"Oh no!!! I see that she is in anguish and mourning, feeling desolate and alone because I am gone…..*no no no* – I have made a terrible mistake! I did not see that the little I could do by visiting her was a comfort to her, and now she feels alone and bereft…..oh what a wrong I have done ….I have deserted her….and she cannot hear me or sense me…For a while I stay around and try to warn the little ones if they are too close to an edge and might fall…and comfort them ….but gradually I have no energy left and I move on….."

This regression helped me understand why my daughter occasionally expressed feeling abandoned by me when there was no reason I could fathom from this current lifetime as to why she would feel that way.

VILLAGE LEADER ..... CANADIAN HUNTER

Village Leader

"I am a strong man…..simple…..but proud of my strength…..I have a good wife, and children……I make things out of wood, and some things with metal attached….I make simple furniture…and carts, and repair houses and roofs after it rains….I helped build the wall around our town…."

"We have heard of trouble…..soldiers who don't belong to any lord….they are coming for us…..they have thrown torches into our village…houses are burning…..women and children are running, screaming…..I have a strong staff….I am good at fighting in our contests every year….I am ready, but they have horses ….and swords…..I am fighting off one of them, and another, but there are many…many blows…and finally I am crushed, and a death blow bashes my head….."

In spirit in the bardo:

"I see that I did all I could….and most of the villagers are dead…and there are many guides here to help us…..it was not so wonderful to be strong….in the end it did not matter, it did not help….."

Canadian Hunter

Perhaps to give us time and space to integrate some of our difficult past life experiences, a soul may choose a relatively conflict free, more restful life. I have always felt drawn by any description of the Canadian woods. Feeling a magnetic attraction to a geographical area can often be a portal to a past experience there. Exploring that attraction led to this regression:

"I am a youngish man, tall and capable, wearing a mixture of linen muslin shirt and buckskin coat and breeches, and I have boots. I am surrounded by woods, clean and full of animals but few people. I am a loner and prefer that. I have a long barreled musket which is vital to me. I rarely use it but always make sure the powder is ready: it is the best defense against a charging bear or wolverine. I know quite well these woods and the creatures here, so usually I am able to avoid any problem encounters. I am always alert for every sound and movement but this is my home. I trap beavers for food and pelts which I use for warmth and trade for the few supplies I need. Once in spring and once in fall I go to a trading post. I listen to news but only to hear if more traders or settlers will be coming this way. I will move on to new territory if there are too many. There are some small native villages in the many miles through which I roam. I keep a good distance. Their men study me and I study them, but they leave me alone. I have several caches where I store powder and pelts but they are well hidden. I rarely stay at one for more than a few days. I prefer to keep on the move, always alert. There is a deep silence in these woods, along with all the multitude of chirpings and rustlings and bird calls and the occasional cracking of branches. I do this through many winters and summers. I am content. I will keep on doing this….."

Moving forward in that lifetime I see that one day when he is much older and has lost some speed, agility and acuity of eyes and ears, he is felled by an arrow despite his vigilance. It finds its mark well and the end is quick. He is content to let go in peace. He takes with him into the spirit world a deep calm and peace.

BLACK MAMA

Prelude

My senior year in college I knew I wanted to change career goals from international diplomacy to psychotherapy. I took classes in Psychology but could only accumulate enough for a minor. To pay for the future education and training I needed, I spent a year getting a teaching credential, figuring that high school teaching would be a good background for doing family therapy. My first teaching job was in a Latino school in south Los Angeles, near the port, just south of predominantly African American areas. I found a soft jazz station on local radio particularly soothing after a stressful day trying to manage 150 restless junior high students. The next year I taught senior high English in a school of mixed races, with some classes of predominantly African American students. Sometime in the spring of that year, I suddenly developed a pronounced aversion to cutting meat, and then to cutting up any food. This was quite disturbing since I had always loved to cook and I cooked most of the meals. My new husband was a good cook and took over for a while. Before too long, I was again able to cut vegetables, on a plastic board, but for months I could not cut meat anywhere and only recently am I again able to cut anything on a wooden board, and even now

I strongly prefer bamboo which has a hardened surface that the knife does not penetrate. Until I did past life regression therapy, this was just an unexplained anomaly to me.

Fear of making a mistake and getting punished has been a theme I had worked on over several regressions and in other therapies, yet it had remained stubbornly persistent in my psyche. So I set resolving that as the goal for the following regression:

"I am a black mama, in a large kitchen, preparing lunch. There is a bowl of fruit ready. I am at a long wooden cutting board where I am chopping pork with what feels like a small hatchet. There is a basin at the end of the board that is used to collect scraps. It is hot and humid and I am mumbling to myself, not happy."

"What are you mumbling, Mammy?" my therapist asks.

"Shouldn' had oughta dun it….shouldn' had oughta dun it…. shouldn' had oughta dun it…."

"Done what?" But no more words come, just a strong sense of disturbance and smoldering anger. Everything feels jumbled. The next thing I know the meat is back in from the cook house and I have a platter of food I am taking outside to the massa' who prefers his lunch outdoors on a slightly raised veranda under the welcome shade of a tree.

"Thank you Mammy…that looks good."

"Humph."

"Now, Mammy, you know how things are……… you'll get over it…."

"I go back to the kitchen and bring out another platter of food....I am sweating with rage and confusion as well as the heat. Something's been forming...has formed in that rage.... I don't want him to keep doing what he does.....I am resolved he's not going to do it anymore...."

"Evening comes, and I am in the kitchen kneading bread for the morning. I look out the window and I can see a building of two rooms. A young slave girl goes in one of the doors, looking scared, followed by the master. I feel cold and hot and clammy at the same time. I take a big butcher knife with me. I go to the building and to that door, wait just a minute, then open it quietly. Sure enough, there he is on top of her, doing his nasty business, making babies to sell. I plunge that big knife deep inside him. He grunts and turns toward me and starts to rise up but then falls back down. The girl wrestles her way out from under him."

"Mammy, wha' yo' dun dere?!! Dey'll kill yo' fer dat! Yo' gots ta getta away from here!"

"But I don't have any plans. I haven't thought ahead at all. I could only mutter over and over that he should not make more babies to sell. The girl goes in the kitchen and quickly gathers some bread and meat and fruit and ties it in a bundle and straps it on me."

"Run, Mammy, run! ....Git as fer from here as yo' can!"

"And she shoos me on my way...... I walk along the road all night but by sunup I am plumb tired. I rest a bit, then walk along a gully in the shade, not very far from the road. I am confused and exhausted and numb............Then I hear them….the eager yelps of the dogs, coming up fast toward me. I start to run, but stumble and fall among the stones and weeds in the gully. The dogs are around me now, barking wildly, and then I hear the voice of the overseer."

"So it WERE you, Mammy….and you thought you could get away with it? How, could you, Mammy? I'd a never believed it of you…but here you are, and now you're a goin' back to face a mighty big meetin'!"

"He puts a rope around my neck and drags me back to the wagon in the road and shoves me up onto it. As the dogs settle in around me I am alternately numb, exhausted and terrified. I see the sky jostling above me."

"Soon enough I am back, and my hands tied around a tree. The top of my dress is ripped off. All the slaves are made to gather and watch, and I sink deep in shame and humiliation. The lash cuts deep and stings mightily, but it is almost a relief because it takes my thoughts off the faces of all my people staring at me with shock and horror, fear and grief. After a long time they untie me and make me face my people. The massa's men are saying something but I can't even hear it, I am so deep in pain and shame and humiliation. After what feels like an eternity in the sun they finally puts a rope over a tree branch and around my neck. "Den I feels it….da deep grief and shock and fear….my folks is terrified and I won' be dere to comfort dem….ah have dun failed dem…." And then the rope lifts me and chokes me and I kick….and then it is over. I die in a wave of shame."

My guide begins the bardo work. "It's over now, Mammy. You can go to the light. Can you see the light?"

"I don' see no light."

"Look for the white light…it is there to comfort and guide you."

"I don' wan' no white light…"

"Mammy! Are you developing attitude? The white light is there to help you…" (The guide senses something, but unclear what) "You need to move into the light now, and leave that pain behind you. You're not there anymore…" But try as she will, I cannot get motivated or see white light.

That particular regression left me feeling very unfinished and ungrounded. It had felt physically overwhelming and exhausting. I was drained. A woman I had felt an instant connection to applied some aromatherapy essential oils to help me feel more grounded and present. That helped some, and so did a nap, but there was still something that felt unfinished. Not uncommonly, especially in training stages and in the early development of Matrix or Deep Memory Process regression therapy, a powerful regression would feel impossible to complete in one session. There might be residual body symptoms that needed body work or a rigid belief that had been substantially shaken loose but needed repeated positive mantras to replace it. In our training workshops we had scheduled follow up sessions for that purpose.

I started the follow up work where I had left off. Mammy couldn't or wouldn't move into the white light. Roger Woolger came to assist. "Try a gold light…that is powerful for many Buddhists".

A gold light did not work either, but I did begin to see a red light.

"Ask for a guide figure appropriate to you, Mammy" Roger suggested.

Right away I saw a thin elderly black woman. She seemed to be chanting something, and she had around her a crowd of black people, swaying to the rhythm of her chant. I leaned closer to hear.

"Ya gotta' go to da HEART…ya gotta' go to da Heart…..ya gotta' go to da HEART….."

I joined the crowd and began to sway to her rhythm. I noticed we were gathered by the side of a river, with some flashes of silver in the sunlight, or maybe an energy stream. After we had fallen very much in rhythm together she changed the chant slightly with a new emphasis:

"ya gotta go TRU da heart ….ya gotta go TRU da heart….ya gotta go TRU da heart….."

She began to lead us in a line that snaked along the shore, all moving forward and swaying with the rhythm of the chant. After some minutes of this she led the line to the water's edge and across the water to the other side, and me with them, still chanting in rhythm. We seemed to walk on air, and yet it felt steady beneath us. I felt a deep release and peace as I got to the other side, and sensed that I had let go of a great deal.

In the bardo state I realized that these black folk were the parents of other children the master had sold, and they had not been able to fully transition beyond this life while that terrible injustice continued. They were the chorus of voices that had entered my head and goaded me to plot to stop the master, and later to plunge my butcher knife deep in his back. Together we had committed murder for justice, to stop the ongoing horror of our young children sold down river into slavery. It was the subliminal echo of their voices that made it impossible for me to cut meat on a wooden cutting board since I had taught a high school English class that was mostly black students, some very articulate. Neither could all the energy of those parents be released until I had come to consciousness and peace about this harrowing occurrence. The wisdom of the old black spirit woman guide knew that we all had to move into heart energy, wrap ourselves in that and heal our hearts, releasing grief and anger and remorse through chanting and moving in the heart energy, before we could move on from that lifetime.

This marked another lifetime I had been significantly influenced by entities. Later I was to discover earlier lifetimes that developed the openness to this, as Hohn, then the Seer on Crete, and the Polynesian shaman.

AUSTRIAN PEASANT REVOLT LEADER

This was a lifetime that has come to me in flashes over the years, referred to earlier as the man who starved in prison. A fondness for rich colored warm brown woods with gold tones, particularly an armoire and a desk I see clearly but have not found in this life, and nostalgia for a country lane lined with poplar trees where I used to ride my horse would come to me from time to time. A startling scene of starving in a dark dungeon with rats came to me at the end of a short regression exercise with Brian Weiss, and further regressions revealed that I was an aristocrat in the 1700's in Austria where I came to believe in more fairness for the peasantry. I helped them stage a protest and revolt of sorts. This did not sit well with a cousin of mine, who maneuvered to have me arrested and kept in a manor dungeon pending a trial, which never happened. It was not easy to kill or have put to death a fellow nobleman with impunity, so he resorted to this long delay tactic….. very long, since I was still in my prime and took a good while starving, getting gnawed by rats and eventually succumbing to cold and pneumonia.

Past lifetimes can affect our body in this life time in many ways: with scars or vulnerable areas that tend to repeated injury or weakness, proclivities toward illness, sensitivities and/

or allergies, defensive or other postural habits, similar facial features, affinities or revulsions toward temperatures or weather conditions, fondness for foods and styles of music, etc., etc. Just about any condition could potentially be a carryover, including good health or health issues.

In this lifetime I was born healthy. My devoted mother was a neonatal nurse who was unfortunately not able to breastfeed. Everything she knew how to do did not keep me from screaming so desperately that she took me to the pediatrician, who came out into the busy waiting room of fussing babies to find the one with that penetrating scream.

"This baby is starving!" he informed my mother. "I know infant screams and this one is feeling desperate for food."

"But I give her a bottle regularly and when she wants one and she drinks the whole bottle but the screaming doesn't stop."

"Then her digestive system isn't mature enough to assimilate the food. We need to slow it down with phenobarbital until she matures." This was pediatric best practice in the early 1950's.

Thus I was kept sedated on phenobarbital for the first year of my life, with dosages increased when screaming returned. To this day I have trouble assimilating what nutrients I need, and most of my health issues have had to do with deficiencies – in vitamin A for skin, B6 and B12 to remedy numbness in hands and elsewhere, C for a weak immune system, minerals for cramps, adrenal hormones for a weak adrenal system, and always I test deficient for enzymes. One day it occurred to me during a water massage that a good way to stave off hunger pangs if no food was available would be to stop craving food....

hunger pants come partly from the promptings of enzymes and digestive fluids as well as brain signals....all my life I have fantasized about food, snuck into the kitchen to get food between meals, crammed my cupboards and refrigerator so full it was hard to find things, and dreamed about banquets. I have struggled with excess weight but never been obese because I am also driven to keep moving to stay warm, which I learned a few years ago is the result of insufficient adrenal hormones. Not too long after all these realizations coalesced with proper hormone replacement, magic happened, as it often does when we sufficiently resolve a past life issue. In this case, I came upon a meal replacement powdered drink mix that included abundant protein, enzymes, probiotics, essential fatty acid omegas, and phytonutrients, almost predigested! Wow...a drink that left me feeling calm, clear and.....what is this new sensation.... could this be what is called satiation, where you feel actually nourished and not just bloated?!!! At last, a meal in a bottle that satisfies!!! I still like food very much but I no longer have any need to overeat, as long as I have one of these drinks every day. And I no longer have food fantasies running constantly at the back of my mind.

I have also learned to deal calmly with the rats that are part of country living for me....

So why doesn't my body just produce all the enzymes it needs, now that I have worked to resolve the hunger issue....? Very often, issues are tied together. I have always had fears of cold and starvation and feeling hemmed in, which I think are partly from the long prison term. I came to understand those fears are entwined with resentment toward the cousin who put me there, and resentment for the loss of youth and good times and life. That resentment was laced with frustration and helplessness – after all, I had long months and years to seethe. It has taken considerable reflection in this life, with knowledge and skills I have now but didn't have then, to realize I could have made good use of all that time alone and privation, to develop mental skills such as meditation among others. I could have developed the power to generate peace and well being…. hindsight 20/20.

I think I made a determination never again to find myself in like circumstances. (The old thought, "If I ever get out of here…..") … but how to accomplish that without having new wisdom and skill? One way, if you want to avoid the noose or prison or burning at the stake or starvation, is to come into a life where you have all you need externally yet are too anxious and too prone to illness – too weak or lacking in adrenal reserves – to fall into any temptation to stick your neck out for justice…..hmmm, seems like just what I have done. So maybe I don't want to be completely hale, hearty and strong, and then feel more responsibility to stand up for others…..maybe in this life I just want to work on healing myself from the patterns and traumas of many lifetimes and helping others quietly as a healing assistant. (I very much believe the power to heal comes from the healer within us, so the best therapist or teacher or healer is at most an assistant).

ATLANTEAN HERBALIST FORGIVEN

Having worked on several past life experiences, I decided I wanted to be able to forgive myself for my original error in Atlantis, so that maybe I could prevent any more painful lives of learning derived from it, and regain the ability to learn and know vicariously, through compassionate witness or participation in other people's experiences, rather than having to suffer everything myself. There is a law of karma but there is also a law of grace, which supersedes the law of karma. That is, the grace of forgiveness can lift us out of karma. We still need to learn our lessons but we may be able to learn them differently, through insight and compassion for others. But in order to make this shift we have to be able to forgive others and to forgive ourselves, in order to receive the forgiveness that the Universe/God/Source offers to us. That process for arriving at self- forgiveness may be individual according to a person's belief system but the basic principle is universal. We have to extend forgiveness to others and to ourselves in order to receive forgiveness. This is the metaphysical principle given to us in the Our Father prayer from Jesus: "Forgive us our debts as we forgive our debtors" applies to forgiving ourselves as well as others. It can be hard to forgive ourselves until we feel we have received forgiveness, but it can also be hard to receive forgiveness until we can forgive ourselves. As I watched my soul story evolving through past life regressions, I realized I was caught in this conundrum of guilt.

I went to another week long training that I knew would involve exchanges of regressions, this one at Mt. Madonna yoga retreat center in the Santa Cruz Mountains in California. I set my intention firmly and spent much of the night awake praying both to receive forgiveness and to forgive myself. When my turn for regression came I was paired with a fellow therapist I trust deeply and feel a strong past life bond with. I began by reviewing what I could remember from my herbalist life in Atlantis. I saw that even though I did get assigned to fill at least part of the role of the woman I murdered, I never did radiate light as I had imagined I would and in fact began to decline quickly from fear of the repercussions of my actions, because I knew in that early life about the Law of Karmic return but nothing of the law of forgiveness or grace, and I became increasingly fearful of what might happen to me. Moving forward in that life I saw myself holding a mirror that was cracked, and I froze into that moment, with a mixture of feelings of terror and shame. I knew I had gone insane. I felt stuck there and could barely hear anything my therapist said.

A trainer named Eve came to help and asked "What sound would that feeling make?" Almost involuntarily I began to shriek a cry of the damned and the thought came "a bat out of hell" and I then realized I was indeed a bat. I could feel my wingspan... I saw a figure a little distance away – a man dressed in flowing dark robes with dark hair and beard and a turban on his head. I flew to him. I found myself hanging upside down clinging with my claw feet to the forearm of this man I intuited to be Christ. I could feel the scaly texture of my claw feet and the hair along my sinewy legs. I felt such relief in finding myself there that I could not move. I felt such love from this figure, and as the bat I could let in the waves of compassion from him. I knew I had finally been released and come home and I was profoundly grateful. I poured out love to my Savior and for once felt truly open to receiving His Love. I was so moved by this transformation that I clung to that arm – I did not want this profound connection to end. I could not or would not move for a long time, perhaps half an hour while the room slowly cleared as other sessions ended and everyone went to lunch. I was bathed in bliss. Finally I felt that I needed to let my partner get to lunch so I reluctantly let go.

This regression as the bat redeemed by the Christ figure emanating love definitely ranks as one of the top five peak experiences of my life, along with giving birth to my three children. Since this transformative experience I have been able to relax at a profound level, far more than simply the physical/emotional/mental level I was already proficient at. It has brought me a deep spiritual peace that has allowed me to slowly gain confidence in myself as a beloved creature of a loving Creator. Levels of anguish I didn't even know I had as I went about my active life have just drained away. I still have work to do training my body and mind to step out of survival mode and deeply instill in myself a wellness mode – the optimal functioning of mind and body that are free to respond fully to every moment, not entrenched in the past nor worrying about the future. But anytime I revive and relive this memory I have what I need to rise above any dark cloud. I can feel confidence in the continuity of my life stream beyond this lifetime, and I can see past any horrors going on in our world, to feel the "ok-ness" of life, to say with mystic Julian of Norwich who received in a vision of Christ the message: "All is well....and all shall be well....and all manner of things shall be well."

Reflecting on this I do not know why the Christ figure appeared in dark robes with a turban. I have certainly never seen a picture of Christ that looked like that. Perhaps it was a disciple of Christ that emanated Christ love. What I do know is the overwhelming feelings of this experience, and I am forever grateful for the gift of them continuing to work in my life. Psychologist Carl Jung spoke of the "numinous" in dreams and sometimes in life, referring to visions and experiences filled with bright energy we recognize as something well beyond the ordinary joys and high points in our lives. As for the experience of being a bat, I think my psyche expressed through a momentary archetypal possession by the symbol of the bat the truth of how I felt at a deep level – like a bat just released from hell.

HOHN

Before I did any assisted past life regressions I did a full cycle of Shamanic seasonal training – 13 weekly sessions each for spring, summer, fall and winter plus workshops, over a two year period, with a Jungian oriented licensed clinical social worker/psychotherapist who was also a shaman trained in the Cherokee tradition of her grandmother as well as having trained under Michael Harner, Carlos Castaneda and his protégé who developed Soul Retrieval work, Sandra Ingerman. I wanted to do a soul retrieval and set up a session. I had already done the 2 years of journeying, the shamanic practice of exploring the lower world and upper world (middle world being our normal space time frame on this earth) so I was quite comfortable opening to my unconscious in the altered state induced by drumming. I knew and trusted this shaman so I thought the soul retrieval session would be productive.

A good shaman tunes into and follows the instructions of his/her guides, sometimes despite the wishes and conscious intentions of the recipient of a healing. In this case, I lay next to the shaman for well over half an hour while she tuned in to her guides and intermittently smiled and chuckled. At the end of that time she told me that the guides had informed her that she was not to do a soul retrieval on me that day. She must have

A Labyrinth of Lifetimes

told them she needed to do something for me since I had come to her and paid her for this experience. So she did a healing on my liver/gallbladder area, which did sometimes cramp and ache at night which I had never mentioned to her. Then she told me the one thing that the guides had given her permission to share with me: "You have an enormous, at least 12 foot tall, polar bear guarding your root chakra." What I took away from this session was increased respect for this shaman and her work, that she was faithful to her teaching and training and did not cave in to the pressure of producing to meet expectations.

Fast forward, to a time after I had experienced 6-8 past life regressions either directly with Roger Woolger or under his supervision. I had participated in some local one day workshops of holotropic breathwork, developed by famed psychiatrist Dr. Stanislaus Grof. This modality consists of lying down with an assisting partner sitting supportively at your side but not usually intervening, while you listen to loud pounding music and breathe in a deep rhythmic pattern that triggers an altered state. You follow your visions or experience wherever it takes you, sometimes into deep emotional release. I was participating in a weekend holotropic intensive in a serene mountain setting. I had finished my session and was laying down just resting when I felt a strong cramping in my chest. I briefly wondered if I could be having a heart attack but then intuitively knew these were spasms of grief. It felt like someone (or more than one) other person's grief. Then I spontaneously felt myself to be a somewhat primitive but powerful man, surrounded by people drumming. My heart was feeling regret about the deaths of several people, and I was feeling the grief of those people who had lost their lives. Intuitively I understood that this was a shaman from a very icy Nordic land who had caused the deaths of these people, and subsequently lost his own life while on a shamanic journey surrounded by his tribesmen who were drumming. He had left his body through his root chakra and not been able to return. I suddenly understood why my body has the quirk of my tailbone and sitz bones going cold and my inability to warm them without some external source of heat, despite being able to warm my hands and feet. I had asked various doctors and healers for a solution to this riddle but no one had been able to explain it to me. Connecting with this powerful primitive shaman was alarming to me and I broke out of the regression. But that left me feeling so ungrounded and scared that a couple of days later I arranged for my friend who organized the holotropic breathwork sessions to sit with me to provide a safe container and grounding while I worked through the regression. I knew I had to do this because of alarming turns in my psychotherapy practice. I normally prefer to avoid dealing with suicidal patients and usually manage to attract courageous, tenacious patients who do not go that route no matter how horrible the traumas they have lived through. But when I came home from the holotropic breath workshop I suddenly found no fewer than SIX of my patients struggling with suicidality!

I easily slipped back into the connection with this Nordic shaman, who told me his name was Hohn. His name was more of a sound than a recognizable name, and he wore a bone through his nose. I was able to feel that while he was powerful and menacing he did not really intend evil. His job was to protect his village from unseen forces and help them with whatever crises presented themselves. It was to the village's benefit if he acquired more power to do so. When he sensed intruders into his people's territory, he would manipulate forces to cause them to have accidents or send them telepathic suggestions to become lost and confused and die in the cold. Then he would gather power from their mental and emotional bodies. But that meant he would also gather their distress and grief at their plight, which he would compartmentalize away in his psyche so it would not disturb his power. But on one occasion while his soul was roaming in an altered state journey, he came under the influence of a shaman more powerful than himself that did something similar to him, causing him to become lost and confused, unable to return to his body which then died. He had come to learn more about the nature of power and how it is to be used, partly through his study of Christ through his connection with me, because he can listen when I listen or read. He now regretted his abuse of his victims and appealed to me to help them regain a more full connection to their souls. I have no idea if my patients were reincarnations of his victims; I only know that as I worked with them to regain their heart strength and courage and set aside suicidal impulses, this sense of urgency from Hohn dissipated. He still gave me an eerie feeling and I even made a mask of him to try to externalize him – get him out of my energy field. The mask sits in my office to this day. However, I understood that the help went two ways: he and his polar bear power animal had watched over me and protected me, I sensed through many lifetimes.

Was I Hohn? Or was he an entity attached to me? I knew that entities can be attached to a person over many lifetimes, often connected to a particular body part. I understood that I had a role to play in helping Hohn evolve, and introducing him to Christ so he could then relate to Jesus more directly. Why it works this way, indeed even how it works, I don't fully understand. I just know we are invited and requested to help others find Christ energy in whatever way we are guided to do that. Sometimes the way is simple kindness without even words; sometimes the way is indirect or mysterious. I am grateful to those who have helped me and I know it helps us all when we become channels of light for others.

Normally when an entity no longer attaches to you, the body part that may be involved heals, unless that body part stores further residues from other lifetimes. I still struggle with cold tailbone and sitz bones on occasion (my husband used to refer to me as "Ice butt" when I would ask him to spoon behind me so I could finally sleep). But I did finally meet a chiropractor who explained that my problem could be a failure of the triple heater – the most mysterious of the meridians because it does not correlate to any specific organs. When the triple heater runs out of energy, this cold ensues. He told me I could relieve the cold by mechanically pumping muscles, which does work somewhat but is tiring. Since I discovered I had probably always struggled with intermittent adrenal insufficiency, I view this cold as a symptom of that lack, and it is definitely improved since I take adrenal supplements. This is an example of how mind, body, soul and spirit are interrelated and often we need to give a condition physical as well as psychological attention and correction.

SORCERER'S APPRENTICE/VICTIM – BLACK BIRD

For some years when I was young, maybe about ages 8 or 9 to 12, I used to see the dim outline of a large black bird sitting on the fence outside my window, a hypnagogic image that would come as I was falling asleep and it would startle me awake. I would lie awake frozen with fear for a while, and then out of exhaustion finally fall asleep without the bird appearing again (or image, if it was that, but it seemed more real than an image, yet the couple of times I managed enough courage to get up and check, there was no real bird outside my window and none had flown away.) Mostly I just shut my eyes and lay very still, hoping the bird could not see me. I used that image as induction to this regression:

"I live in a mountain forest. We live in a craggy area nestled against a mountain, with trees around us that hide us from view. I am kind of an assistant….more like a serving boy, to a shaman that has not yet decided whether to take me on as an apprentice. If he decides he is willing to take me there will be some kind of initiation to test whether I am right for the job of helper student."

"He explains very little, mostly has me fetch things or hold something or prepare herbs, strip bark and boil wood, or cook food. I spend time hunting for animals and plants. He feeds animals that are drawn to him, large and small. Sometimes I find them dead…but many animals in the forest die….Sometimes the shaman is gone, I don't know where. But there is an eerie presence about the place when he is gone. I am a little afraid of him, but even more anxious when he is gone, because of that eerie presence. I can't see who or what it might be. I don't have anybody else. I hardly remember my parents, only that one night there was a lot of noise and fighting and when I ran outside I saw fires everywhere. A neighbor told me to run away very fast. I did, and when I looked back from the top of the hill, our village was in flames. I ran until I couldn't run anymore, and saw a cottage in a field. I asked for food there. The lady took me in and fed me. Then she wanted me to gather sticks for kindling, which I did. The next day her man came to the cottage, pulling a hand cart with heavy sacks. He wanted me to unload the sacks but I couldn't do it; I stumbled and fell under the weight. He hit me with a stick. The woman asked him to stop. He did. I was hungry. Every day he told me to do something I wasn't big enough to do and he would hit me when I couldn't do it. I was still very hungry but finally one night when they were asleep I snuck out from my place along the cottage wall and took off along the path the cart had come on. I walked and walked until I finally saw a little village, a little before dawn. I hung around outside a tavern/mill/bakery/inn/drinkhouse. I was very hungry. Finally a man came out and saw me and gave me some old bread and some water. He wanted me to gather wood so I did. He let me sleep on the ground just inside the door to his inn. He had me stir gruel in a pot and gather wood and dead leaves and brush."

A Labyrinth of Lifetimes

"One day there was a man passing through the village. He wore a cape. People seemed afraid of him but they didn't talk to him or talk about him. He watched me for a while. Then he said something to the innkeeper. Then the innkeeper told me I could not stay at the inn anymore and I was to go with the man with the cape. We walked a very long way through fields, then up through hills and then steeper and steeper paths until we came to this rocky place under the trees, where I am now. I have been here for years now, and still the old man says very little to me."

"Sometimes there is a large black bird that sits on a lower branch of one of the tall trees near us. I suppose it is an owl even though it doesn't look like any owl I have seen before. It often seems to be watching me."

"I am tired of being here and lonely. I think about running away but I don't want to be hungry again. The old man seems to know I think about leaving. Some days he makes me go off a little ways but stay in sight. He handles things on a crude table he has, and mutters in an odd voice but I can never hear clearly what he is saying."

"I am older now, bigger and stronger. Not as strong as the old man, but I can see that one day I will be. He still doesn't teach me very much, but watches me. I don't like the way he watches me. I think more about leaving but some force stops me before I can ever go or even prepare to go. I don't know what it is. And always that black bird seems to be watching me, especially when the old man is not around. The bird's eyes are keen and piercing. I think I would like to throw a rock at the bird when the old man is not around, but when I think that, I can't pick up a rock. In fact I can't even seem to do anything. I seemed to be fastened down in place, and find it hard to breathe."

"One day there is a new look on the old man's face and I shudder. I don't know what it means. Only that I feel more and more that I have to get away..and more times when I am not able to move, even when the old man is nearby. I don't know why I can't move. I'm scared. Somehow this seems the old man's doing. I am more and more afraid. Sometimes I can't breathe. I don't know what is happening."

"One day the eerie presence and the old man and the black bird seem to come closer and closer and I sense something is happening but I don't know what. I can't move at all now. I open my mouth to yell but no sound comes out....no one could hear me anyway."

"There is something about to happen that feels evil.....I don't know what it is....I can't talk...."

....at this point my regression guide calls Roger to come assist and briefly explains the situation.

"Ahh, dark magician" Roger surmises. "Remember you can always call for the help of a white magician..."

"He sees I am terrified, feel unable to do anything...." "The Christ light magician is always stronger than the dark one," he reassures me.

"Somehow hearing that relieves a knot of terror in me. It also breaks the regression and I feel too weak, too exhausted to continue it. It seems enough to know I am safe, here and now."

A Labyrinth of Lifetimes

This was an episode that was never fully resolved for me. To this day I ponder whether the shaman/magician was truly evil or whether the day for an initiation had finally arrived and I just had too much fear to pass through it. My strong intuitive sense is that the black bird was the familiar of the shaman, and the shaman could send him to watch me and gain information from the bird. But he never granted me any explanation of that.

Note: as I write this, two birds are copulating at the top of a tall Leylandi Cypress at the top of the hillside above my window. Hawks? Neither bird is black, and they are not watching me, but still…..a very rare sight, one I have never seen in 30 years of living here…….synchronicity? I will take it as an omen that Life replaces fear and darkness.

SEER IN CRETE

I had done several week long trainings and more than a dozen exchange regressions as well as my individual regression therapy. I was (overly) confident that I had already been through the most intense regressions and future regressions should be smoother and easier. Roger began with an entry into regression that imagines an airplane trip around the world. You observe lands that you fly over in a north to south or east to west or any direction you choose. You might fly around the world and return to the spot that had the most energy for you, or go directly to a country if you feel a strong pull. I went to some place in the Middle East that I sensed was ancient and would not correspond to any modern map.

I saw myself as a child playing with beautiful gemstones but they were not mine and I was not rich. With such a benign beginning I anticipated maybe being apprenticed to a jeweler, although I was a girl. So I was a little puzzled when the regression did not flow at all with my novice therapist-in-training guide. This was not usually a problem for me, though it is a common problem for others. Roger had told me my memories were unusually close to the surface, and my past life stories generally flowed freely. This time felt like it would be pleasant and mild, starting from an attraction to gem stones…..I did really like

A Labyrinth of Lifetimes

those stones, which looked like ruby, lapis lazuli, malachite, amber.......but that was all that would come.

In the next general session, I tried to listen to Roger along with the rest of the group, but found myself dazed and spacey and teary. I began to feel queasy and afraid and a little dazed. I must have looked out of it because Roger looked at my face and said softly:

"You do know these are not your feelings from now, don't you?" (He knew my usual demeanor from many previous trainings).

I nodded dumbly, with growing terror. Actually all I knew was that I could hear Roger's voice and I trusted him....

"Do you want to let that go?" I nodded, but found I couldn't speak at all...try as I might, nothing would come out....

"Ok, let's see what this is...."

As soon as I could feel the support of his full presence, images began to flood my mind. I could see I was a little girl who loved to play with the beautiful stones, like being given candy. But they were used as a treat by two women who manipulated me and terrified me. I was in their service from a young age, and they kept me isolated in a kind of quasi-religious center. As I got older I had to inhale a kind of smoke that made me drowsy and spacey and I would see images I could not control and sometimes beings next to me that scared me and talked to me. The most upsetting was when they talked through me. I had to do this often, and I was not the only one. People with money would come and pay the two old women and then I would have to provide this service. Afterwards I would feel nauseous and anxious, and they would give me the stones to play with to calm my nerves. I would fixate on the beautiful colors of red and blue and gold and green. I wanted to leave that place, to get away, but they threatened that if I tried to do that, a powerful and terrifying man would take my soul and keep it and I would never get it back. This totally unnerved me more, so I was stuck in that dilemma.

All during this regression I could barely talk at all, I felt so spacey and I felt this girl's fear at being discovered talking, very much afraid the two old women would find out I was talking to a helpful stranger that had not gotten their permission or paid their price.

I finally I managed a tiny whisper, "They'll hear," motioning to Roger to be quiet.

Roger's soft voice "What will they hear?"

"Us…"

"Who are they?"

"The old women….the ones who make me sit in the smoke and talk to the men."

"What do you talk to them about?"

"I don't know….whatever comes out….I never know what will come out….."

"And when you first came here….Where did you come from?"

"I don't know…..it seems like I've always been here…"

"Tell me about where you are…."

A Labyrinth of Lifetimes

"Shh, they might hear us...."

"What are you afraid will happen if they hear us?"

"They might let the scary man take away my soul.......Can I play with the stones now, pretty stones..."

"What stones?"

"The pretty ones they give me to play with, sometimes, when they are happy with me.....the same ones they let me hold when I first came here.... pretty stones, blue, red, green, yellow......."

Suddenly I hear children screaming as the scene shifts. Then I realize I am screaming, and I hear many children...

I begin to hear babies screaming, at first at a distance and then closer and closer, all around me. I begin screaming their screams and can not stop for a good while. After a good deal of intense energy has come through me, I begin to see that I am on the water, on the ocean a little way out from the shore, in a dugout boat. I am an old man, but strong. I am the village shaman, and I am doing what I can to help.

"I am screaming......I can't express all their screams fast enough, ...until suddenly all goes quiet."

Roger: "What is happening now?"

"....it's dark, nighttime......I think all the children are dead... a great tidal wave......I did what I could for them......I held all the young children close to me in a boat, because I knew their parents could never run fast enough with them, so I told them just to take the babies and older children they could run with and climb up the hills as fast as they could……We had so little warning, the great wave was almost there when I sensed it coming, so little time to wake up and warn the village…… The ones that would be too heavy to carry quickly up the hills I kept with me. I had a wild hope we might get lucky on the sea, but mostly I would protect their spirits while their bodies drowned. I would keep them all in my aura…"

"…but I couldn't stop the little ones' fear, just keep them close in my energy so they wouldn't be lost and alone…..they have been with me ever since….."

Roger: "We have a lot of helpers here who can help the little ones find their parents…..would you like them to help with that?…….I feel for the energy of what he says, and feel a lot of light in the room….."

"Yes, …help the little ones……I feel so very tired now, such a long time holding so many so close….I am so tired now….."

"You rest, old man….and I want to return now to the girl with the stones…..Kathy, can you find your way into the bardo with this girl?"

"Yes…..but she was a woman as well as a girl when you were talking to her….split between the two…"

Can you tell us more about her?

"She was used by people who wanted to make her a kind of seer, kept often in a drugged state by being placed where she had to breathe vapors, very afraid when not in that state, and then the only thing calming was playing with the stones, when they would let her. It was what they used to pacify her when

A Labyrinth of Lifetimes

she was first brought there as a young child…..she thought at times of running away, wanted to, but had nowhere to go and they kept her terrified that the man who visited sometimes could take her essence, her energy away with him………"

"…. not sure why I flipped into the other lifetime, as a south sea island village shaman, but the two lives just feel very connected …."

This regression was intermingled with that of the south sea shaman, for which further bardo work and reflection follow…..

SHAMAN IN POLYNESIA

I could see that I was an older man, shaman for this village. It was already night, with the moon climbing. I had so little warning. I got a sudden sense of something coming, danger. I looked carefully all around. I detected a small trembling in the waves. I knew this could mean a great wave coming. I hurriedly warned several of the strongest men and women to gather what babies they could carry and what children could run with them up into the mountain. The rest of the young ones we put on a few boats with some strong row-men who had no children, in the slim hope the sea would be kind and we could by magic ride out the wave. I gathered several young ones who could not walk far and went in one of the outriggers. By now the water was running out from shore, a sign the great wave would come soon. We managed to get most of the few boats in the water, mine included. I gathered the frightened children close to me. I had a sense the sea would soon claim us, so I connected to the life force of each child, to steady it and ready it for the passing. But one child I could not manage to calm and he began to scream, more and more wildly. One by one the calm broke in the others and they joined in his screams. The great wave was visible now, racing toward us. With everything in me I held to the calm and the harmony so we would pass peacefully into the next realm and the little ones would know they were secure with me as we entered the kingdom of the deep sea. I could feel them trying to hang on to me but losing themselves in winds of fear and screaming. Our row-man bravely faced into the mountainous wave but the sea goddess would have her own and the wave turned us up, over and down into her realm. I held steady the spirits of the children as best I could but I know there are many still caught up in their terror at the ferocity of the wave and its wind.

For me it was easy to pass into the deep, but for my sacred duty to these little ones, I must keep them close to me. I must stay in the sea and return to the sea to help them, each one, to find their mothers in the spirit realm, to know they are safe and recover harmony. These are the children who cling to me, frantically screaming for their mothers to hear them and know them and reach them, so they can recover calm and rejoin their own spirits.

These were the screams that kept coming out of me, and I couldn't even catch a breath between them, the little ones were so anxious for release. I am aware of kind mothers around me (workshop trainees) who offer to receive the young children and hold them. I scream until there is no breath left in me. I am spent but at last there is calm, and the Sea and I are one, at peace.

I have never been so physically or psychically exhausted after a regression. It took my body energy several days to recover. I was a little sad that my effort to help the children pass calmly into the next realm had not been more successful, but I knew I had done all I could, and finally they had gotten to safety. Because this was a demonstration and we had other things to do and I was totally exhausted and soaked from all the sobbing and sound coming through me, we did not do all the completion work of moving through the rest of this life and its death experience and bardo work in this session.

In our group of therapists were practitioners of many modalities. I did do a therapy session with healing sounds offered by one of the other trainees who was an expert in Sound Healing. She told me that the screams that erupted so forcefully were "authentic screams of terrified pre-verbal children". She offered to do sound healing on me to help me recuperate from that exhausting session, and help harmonize the energies. She intoned sounds into several of my chakras. Her penetrating therapeutic vocalizations seemed to reach right into the chakras along my spine and ease tensions there, and I could feel energies settling. It also felt like holes were filling with strong positive sound vibrations. Still, I was deeply exhausted for at least a week after this session that came from such a deep place. I don't think my subconscious would have allowed this material to surface without the security of Roger's presence and guidance. I have found in my own work that if we respect the subconscious of the person being regressed, that level of being intuitively knows what can be safely worked through.

Reflecting on these two lifetimes over the following days, I came to realize that one life experience enabled the other. That is, the mediumistic experience forced on the seer became a capacity she took with her, though she had little or no control over it. The South Pacific island shaman could put this inherited capacity to better use though he was still limited. He probably received some training from a previous shaman but he only knew how to bind the children's energy to him, not how to help them find their parents again in the afterlife bardo and thus free himself. That does not necessarily mean that no part of each child went freely onto another lifetime, only that fragments of them – especially their fears and experience of the sudden catapult out of body from the tidal wave – stayed bound together with the shaman who did his best to shelter and protect them. One hopes he goes on to learn more about handling life force energy in other lifetimes.

One day some weeks after this I was walking on the pier at the beach a few miles from my home. Something felt different, out of place. Then I realized I had no background thought of plunging into the water. I came off the pier and walked along the water's edge and discovered I had no compulsion to enter the sea. All my life to that point I had an urge to enter water. My mother was a very honest woman but she lied about my age to enroll me in swim lessons (when I was a child the minimum age was supposed to be six). She was alarmed at my urge to jump into water whenever I saw a pool but especially the rare times we went to the beach. I remember getting knocked over by small waves, with salt stinging my eyes and nose and mouth but there was something so magnetic about the water I had to go back in. I have never been suicidal and am fairly cautious about most things, but I have often swum on my own, even in the sea – not recommended, but there are some forces that override all conditioning. This was why the absence of any compulsion to enter the water felt like such a deep shift for me. I can still swim in the ocean (with a warm enough wetsuit!) But I won't swim alone and I have no NEED to swim in the sea; I can swim in a pool that has no magic or allure whatsoever, but is simply a utilitarian and pleasurable way to get exercise.

Sometime later, I returned in meditation to the life of the Woman Seer because I felt a heavy sense of helplessness when I thought about her. I needed to see what became of her in that life. The abusive experiment of trying to "create" a seer by continually forcing her into an altered state did not work very well, and her ramblings to customers who paid the shrine where she worked became less and less decipherable and eventually became gibberish. Eventually she was no use to them so they stopped threatening her with loss of essence and told her to leave the shrine and not come back. She did that, but of course was unprepared for life on her own. She went hungry a lot. Before long she fell ill from exposure and shortly thereafter died. Oddly, she was not afraid in the death process but came to understand that by being ineffective she had actually won – gone free, defeated her oppressors and regained some personal power and sense of self– and she easily let go of her worn out body.

HEALING THE ANCESTORS – IRISH

In some regressions what emerges seems far more likely to be a case of ancestor convergence rather than a past life of the person regressing. In my introduction to Marnie, WW I nurse, I described the example of a co-participant in a workshop who was experiencing strongly the symptoms of what seemed like it would be a past life pilot, but what emerged was a tangle of images, feelings and actions that seemed far more likely to belong to her dead uncle, at least in part. Sometimes there is a mixture of imagery and feelings that may belong to more than one person or lifetime.

Virtually all the indigenous cultures of the world have recognized the influence of ancestors, honored them in some way, feared their intrusion or their disapproval, and/or sought their help or advice. In our current materialistic culture we tend to scoff at these views as superstitious, not possible and certainly not worthy of any scientific exploration. Yet people from traditional cultures tell far more tales than can easily be attributed to coincidence.

In the regression work of Roger Woolger and other therapists, patterns of repeating genetic family stories began to emerge.

Most people are familiar with the idea of alcoholism as an inherited family pattern that has both behavioral and genetic components. But it may well involve the influence of ancestors also, as alcoholics whose vibrational patterns and even astral/desire bodies persist in their alcohol cravings even after bodily death. Those cravings can become attached to vulnerable living members of the family. Clairvoyant psychics tell stories of observing in bars that the astral desire bodies of physically dead alcoholics hang around the familiar atmosphere trying to satisfy their cravings vicariously. Occasionally one will be seen inside the aura of a person who has drunk to the point of blackout and then is seen to merge with that person. Now the alcoholic has a new problem – a new source of cravings and thoughts – powerful suggestions of where and how to drink more, until that person eventually succumbs to death. This could happen with a departed alcoholic relative also. That is, not all of the being would have departed to the higher spirit realms.

Incest is another family pattern that could involve the influence of ancestors, perhaps without any direct genetic component, but rather just the influence of issues never resolved. Those can generate thought-feeling-behavior complexes that don't entirely vanish with physical death. If they are strong and there is a family magnetism of other family members who share those complexes, potentially powerful vibrational echoes or even willful desires from the departed can strengthen a complex, in this case a proclivity toward incest, perhaps through suggestion "hanging in the air" or vibrating in the field of the family energy. Incest victims often report acute discomfort with a physical place, for example a house or other venue, where incest is prevalent or where it has taken place.

A Labyrinth of Lifetimes

They are sensitive to the "vibes" of the place, not just associated memories, and this sensitivity can become like radar that alerts them to other potentially hazardous places where similar incest has taken place.

There are many other family patterns that are not so deeply dysfunctional but still have significant impact on family members, and may not even have been recognized as family patterns or in some cases even held up proudly as a mark of distinction. For example, there are military families who proudly lose a son to war in several successive generations. It is hard if not impossible to separate out and assess the strength of different variables potentially involved: genetic disposition to fighting, parental expectation and overt or implied suggestion, a military cultural milieu, a young man's need to rise up to expectations to prove himself a man by "proudly serving", among others. Ancestors may interfere either to reinforce this pattern if they are still caught in the complex themselves even after physical death, or sometimes an ancestor intervenes to try to stop the pattern by haunting a vulnerable son with counter suggestions that generate or exacerbate deep conflict, in an attempt by spirit to break the pattern. Many psychics have commented that one key component of the resistance to the war in Viet Nam was the reincarnation of so many men whose lives were cut short in WWII and who returned in the baby boom which occurred after the war. Those boys born in the late 40's and early 50's would have come of age in the 60's. "Hell no, I won't go" was a slogan that gained momentum in that decade. That was a case of many spirits determined to break a widespread human pattern, but a similar phenomenon can happen on a small scale within an individual family. The more psychically open family member who exhibits the conflict may be the one who shows up for past life regression therapy because they sense the influence of "someone else" in their dreams or their thoughts or decision making process.

Other patterns that run in families as inherited "coincidences" can seem like a curse or a charmed existence. The Kennedys are a famous example of the "curse" that seems to doom some family members to early violent death, especially if they engage in public service. Even in 2020 two Kennedy grandchildren drowned when their sailboat capsized in a storm. Ted Kennedy was discouraged by family and others and did not run for president or die early but his career was overshadowed by the tragic drowning of his girlfriend Mary Jo Kopeckne which many people attributed to Ted (and his drinking) and the family cloud. Philandering is another common family pattern, especially among men but also women in some cases. On the surface it can be explained by learned cues and implicitly or explicitly accepted behaviors that take on the power of suggestion. But some folks who try various methods of therapy for breaking that pattern have found ancestral involvement to be a significant factor. Workaholism is another pattern that can have ancestral components as well as patterning that is overtly passed from generation to generation.

Sometimes there is a pattern that does not seem to involve learned behavior at all. In my own case, when I looked at my family tree, I saw a pattern of losing a boy child in four generations, which was as far back as we were able to trace family records, due to the burning of records in Ireland and the Penal Code laws against keeping records. (The British used the lack of records to facilitate their dispossessing families of ancestral land and homes.) My great grandmother lost a son and my grandmother lost her first born son when he was two years old and he fell into the East River in New York. My mother was a pediatric nurse who had run a neonatal unit, but her first born son died of crib death at ten weeks even though she came into the room when she heard him cry and administered CPR right away when she found him suddenly not breathing. That was the most important unresolved event of her life, which haunted her thoughts in later years even as she approached death in a nursing home. I was nervous when my first son was born but things seemed ok until my third child, a daughter, was born. Then I began having haunting thoughts that one of my children would die. I tried everything to push away these forebodings and thought I had succeeded until my second son was killed when a car ran over his bicycle right near his school. My mother's brother also lost his three year old first son to a sudden infection and my cousin lost his oldest daughter at 18 years old to an ear infection that went to her brain. These were all in big cities with modern hospitals.

When I looked for the roots of this pattern through ancestor regression therapy what came up strongly was the Irish aversion to doing grief work and the way that can have and did have an impact on our family. The Irish are known for their custom of holding a wake, which usually involves significant drinking and telling stories and jokes, sometimes with gallows humor. When my father died my mother was very disapproving of any tears I shed – she saw these as a lack of faith that my father was in heaven. She told me the Irish Catholic view is somewhat like the Gypsy view: in life you will have troubles, but rejoice when a good person has died because they are now safe and comfortable in heaven. Family seemed to be mixed with culture because I got a clear sense that the Irish famine was an important if indirect factor. As far as I know, no one in my direct lineage died in the famine, but death and grief were all around them. Up to one in four Irish people did die directly or indirectly from the famine – whole families were found starved to death in their homes, others sent all their children to die in the churches. And up to one in four Irish emigrated, to the United States and other countries. The famine of 1845-50 caused such an epidemic of grief that the Irish people were traumatized for generations and only toward the close of the twentieth century and beyond, along with the Celtic revival, have there been significant national discussions of the impact of the famine and attempts to process that impact. My cousin who lost his daughter never fully recovered even though she was one of eight children. His brother who has nine children is a successful doctor. He made sure all nine of his children had bachelor's degrees and all but one has a master's degree, and all of his brother's seven surviving children have at least bachelor's degrees and many have master's degrees. I remember his recounting that at a family gathering, with a determined satisfaction "Now NO ONE IN THIS FAMILY has any excuse for starving!!" which struck me at the time as an odd thing to say, but when I did my ancestral regression work I understood what he meant. He had been driven by ancestors to protect the descendants from death as much as possible. But the cultural grief patterns had not been well resolved, and the family kept re-visiting childhood death.

Hopefully the grief work I have done since losing my son and the work I have done on healing my family tree and ancestral lineage will be enough to dissipate any energetic pattern that attracts the experience of losing a child due to unresolved grief. And of course we always want to address any other factors we can that are involved in the complex webs of our ancestral and family lines and our intertwining karmas.

One form of adjunctive therapy that can either lead to a past life regression request or provide further processing of an ancestor issue is Burt Hellinger's Family Constellation Therapy, In this modality a group of people are positioned around the subject according to what the subject remembers of family members and their distance or closeness to one another. Places are assigned for family members lost to death or other circumstances, including babies that were aborted or miscarried. Often a form of family subliminal consciousness or even unconsciousness becomes conscious. As people stand in for family members they sometimes receive an intuitive sense about that person or feels they have a message from that person. Unrealized grief issues about missing members may come to the fore. Sometimes a death or a family member is not even known about but an intuitive sense about that person is spoken by someone positioned in the family constellation, and later checking into family history provides verification of that missing or lost person. Bringing all this to consciousness allows healing not only in the subject person but potentially in other family members as well, providing an important dimension to healing the family tree.

ENUF

Though most of the time I am very upbeat and positive, I still experience intermittent dread of scarcity and starvation and occasionally feel shaken and disempowered by anticipated confrontations with certain individuals. I decided to balance these by searching for a lifetime of positive experience that I could use to help counteract and reprogram cellular habit or whatever other factor was involved. I don't believe that just focusing on the positive without exploring our many shadow elements will work by itself, but in conjunction with the extensive inner exploration I had already done, a purely positive experience if I could find one might prove very helpful.

In regression I return to Polynesia, which has a strong call for me. (Recall my grandfather/godfather Neptune and the Oceania shaman who took the toddlers with him to shield them psychically from the tsunami). At this time I find myself sitting tall and strong on the flattened trunk stump of a palm tree. I watch the sea with deep contentment. I feel rooted to this spot and this area, an island with a small village, fewer than one hundred people. These are my people. I am one with the sea and the sand and the sky. I know deeply that all is well. The sea and the land always provide for our simple needs. I am tall and strong. My job or role seems simply to be…..to remain in deep communion with the sea and the sky and the land. Whenever any problem arises in the village, any dispute between family members or neighbors, the people involved come to see me. They sit or stand near me. They may explain themselves or not. Either way they sit or stand near me in quiet stillness when they have finished. The energy they feel from me calms them and they slowly fill with feelings of the ease and harmony that I feel. They see how to resolve their difficulties and they return to the village, working together at whatever was needed. I remain very still, always steeped in and flowing with deep contentment. Whatever I am/We are…..whatever I have/we have…..it is ENUF.

On reflection, I think this was more likely an archetypal experience than a regression, although I could have been one of the villagers who regularly saw this amazing shaman. He seems mythical, larger than life, but then I think he comes from a time far removed from ours, so who is to say he might not actually have had the gifts and capacities he demonstrated.

What I do know is, since this altered state experience, when I begin to get anxious about money or any other kind of sufficiency, or when I begin to feel afraid of someone and disempowered, I have only to return to this experience to begin to calm down almost immediately. It makes me think of Heartmath, the wonderful set of processes for dispelling anxiety by reliving an inspiring moment in our lives. (See the work of Doc Childres and others at www.heartmath.org – a research center in Boulder Creek, California) I can use this experience in a similar way to the heartmath process and it is even more effective because it was such an intense feeling and experience that lasted several minutes and made (or recalled) a deep impression.

BELLAGIO REVISITED: MONK

In Bellagio I started this account of my regression experiences through the Labyrinth of (my) Lifetimes, and now I come full circle....connecting with a past life in meditation.......

"I am still haunted by a yearning....and the sweetness of a feeling......I see the interior garden of a cloister, on a cloudy day. I am pausing in the deeper shade of a corner, just taking this in......feels like a spontaneous prayer of connection..... I want to preserve this moment....but I know I cannot; everything passes....still, it is so sweet I linger here, in this intense sweetness...."

"I am hearing the chanting within me, echoes of our chanting matins a little earlier.....the resonance, even when we are not chanting, a lifting up surpassed only by the Sacred Communion Host of the Blessed One....when our voices are truly one I am transported from this earth......I see the brown robes of my fellow monks but not their faces, with their cowls pulled over their heads, walking slowly, intent on their inner prayers..... is this a glimmer of what heaven feels like? Ah, but then we shall see Him, a Presence so mighty that my heart catches in my throat and my knees are suddenly weak....I think I might die if I saw him...but no, my body would already have passed from me….such immensity is too much…..I come back to my humble walking….my heart is open wide in gladness for this place and my fellow monks who call in this blessed connection through prayer and singing together……I wonder, do they all feel what I have been feeling?"

"I can feel the cold air now, calling me back to the humble earth….soon the bell will ring for breakfast, some bread and tea, listening to sacred Scripture and some guidance……I have no interest in food now, beyond food….. but I know I will enjoy the bread when I sit down….."

Reflections

Although I am not sure this monastery is the same one I visited in Bellagio because the cloister area is different. (see Introduction: A Bellagio Painting) The cloister and most of the monastery may simply have been eliminated as the town encroached around it. I feel sure the original monastery cannot be far from here, and during this monk's lifetime I feel sure that I at least visited and felt inspired in the monastery in Bellagio that looked so familiar to me.

This was by and large a happy peaceful life, where I got to live out to some extent the longing of Miriam (the Hebrew lady who was so taken by the sight of the Master Jeshua that she had a heart attack when she heard he was killed). I also got to experience at leisure the power of chanting. On various occasions sound healing has been very powerful for me. Verbal interactions with other monks were so limited in this monastery setting that it was easy to have good feelings about them – very little chance for ego and personality conflicts to arise for someone genuinely called to this life style. The time frame for this life would have been late 17th or early 18th century. This lifetime helped repair, to some extent, the life of the simple woman who loved the "good man" who was burned as a heretic, and the damage done to her by also being burned at the stake for not denouncing him. This lifetime allowed me to reconnect to the heart of Christianity, living in simple conditions supportive of the mystical life. A monastery is headed by an abbot or prior, an organizational system far removed from religious political fray and any prying eyes of bishops and parish priests. Because the robes were brown and the activities of the monks were mostly prayer, chanting and silent meals, the order of monks was most likely Carmelite, an order that flourished in Spain, France and Italy until the French Revolution. I feel a strong spiritual affinity for the Piedmont and Alpine regions of Italy and Austria. (see A nun in Piedmont, the northwestern section of Italy that has changed nationality back and forth between France and Italy, and where French is commonly mixed with Italian language.)

The lifetime of this monk I now see filled me with renewed spiritual zeal which would develop into courage. That courage and at least a quasi-Christian sense of injustice in the treatment of peasants would lead me to embrace some ideals of 18th century enlightenment, and with the zeal of youth to co-lead an attempted peasant uprising, as the Austrian leader/enabler of a peasant revolt. Unfortunately I didn't carry true spirituality forward with me, so when that peasant uprising collapsed in the death of many peasants and my aristocratic cousin maneuvering to keep me locked up in a local prison until I starved to death, I became very bitter and would have been contemptuous at the idea of Christian resignation to suffering as a pathway to rising above the limits of this world.

A THREAD THAT WEAVES THE STORIES TOGETHER

In Atlantis, I was drawn by the brilliant colors emanating from the woman in the limelight. I did not understand that she had worked to develop herself to the point where she could exude light, nor that some of her apparent radiance was due to other people projecting energy onto her through admiration, as I also was projecting my admiring energy onto her. In her I was seeing the potential inside of me and each one of us, but did not understand that. Nor did I look ahead to foresee the very predictable results of my actions, in terms of human suffering. This was at least in some measure a chosen blindness. One could argue that if we are unconscious of something, we are not really choosing it. But karma makes us responsible for the results of our actions whether we choose them unconsciously or consciously. Of course the resulting damage to our own heart is more severe if we consciously choose to hurt another person, but damage is still there even if we hurt another person through recklessness or carelessness. There are no human "accidents" in karmic law.

Is karmic law therefore cold heartless divine justice? What about divine mercy? Seeing karmic law as cold and heartless is really just another projection of our immature emotions. We may also think a teacher is harsh because the teacher assigns homework so we can absorb the lesson presented in class. When we are not in a fit of pique we can see the justice in that. But the justice of the karmic teacher is even more finely tuned than that. Those who learned the lesson at first glance are not required to do the homework. Those who did not pay close enough attention or who are not yet developed enough to comprehend the lesson at a glance need to learn the lesson through experience. As in any learning, if we do not waste energy resenting and bemoaning and resisting this process, we learn more quickly and easily. Karmic law really just teaches about reality, in ever greater depth. The child learns that when you drop your toy it may break. When you say mean things to your friend she is likely to feel hurt and angry and may withdraw and leave you lonely.

We are all connected on many levels and we are mirrors of each other, so whatever you do to someone else, you do to yourself. This is the basic karmic law, which wisdom teachers have tried through the centuries to help us understand. "Do unto others as you would have them do unto you." A clearer understanding might be: You ARE doing unto others as you will have them do unto you, sooner or later. We cannot escape the repercussions of our actions because we cannot escape our own selves indefinitely. Eventually the call to wholeness and balance asserts itself, as we move far enough out of balance that we fall down into ill health, ill fortune, broken relationships, addictions, etc. We meet ourselves, as Edgar Cayce said, in troubling situations. Even if we successfully extricate ourselves from a particular situation, we are likely to repeat it as a pattern until we have grasped the basic lessons involved. Karma is not a cruel lord despite what we may think: it is simply there to teach us.

A Labyrinth of Lifetimes

So what is the role of divine mercy and grace? What about Jesus who allegedly "saved us from our sins"? This same Jesus said "Take up your cross and follow me" His path is not easy! Yet it is truly a shortcut to the divine for those able and willing to follow him, for he gives a condensed, crash course in karmic understanding.

Edgar Cayce, renowned psychic who did over fourteen thousand recorded trance readings for people in his lifetime, explained the essence of karma as "meeting oneself to know oneself, and know that we are all one". That means, what you do to others, you will yourself experience in some form, so that you can know and understand what you have done in all its ramifications.

In my history in Atlantis I gave poison that killed a woman who was a wife, mother and valued member of the community. I paid part of my debt in that lifetime by generating such intense guilt and shame that I lost my balance emotionally and went insane. I knew I had done wrong and regretted it but that didn't mean I really understood all the effects my actions had on many other people. The woman who died lost her husband through death and he lost her. I experienced partial loss of my Roman husband to the military and loss of my beloved fiancé Cedric when I became a captive slave of Norsemen. This probably echoed in further losses of partners in other lifetimes. Marnie the World War I nurse mourned the loss of hope for a relationship she would never get to know. The woman I murdered lost her children and they lost her. I lost two babies in my Norwegian life when I was married to an older man who was gone much of the time on trading trips. And I lost my nine year old son to a bicycle accident in my current lifetime. This may look like an eye for an eye as a law of karma, which is an old understanding that does have some truth to it, but the truth from an enlightened perspective that sees the infinite intelligence of the creator is that these kinds of events are definitely not designed to blind us or blindside us (an eye for an eye and the whole world will be blind…). Rather, experience is meant to give us understanding of the true impact of our actions. We get to experience the emotions we triggered in another person, ie, grief for grief. This breaks the heart open so that hopefully we will be more kind and compassionate in the future. We get as many experiences as we need in order to develop whatever levels of compassion we have not yet developed. That is one reason it is so useful to meditate on compassion, as the Buddhists do, and practice compassionate service, as many true Christians do.

These are ways we may be able to develop a compassionate heart without having to personally experience in detail every suffering we have triggered. Instead we may learn the effects of our actions by experiencing them vicariously through compassionate attention to the sufferings of others.

As the Atlantean herbalist I misused my craft and medical knowledge to kill. As an herbalist in the Middle Ages I was burned at the stake. In this lifetime I have struggles with allergies to many plants. It was my exasperation at non-stop sneezing that first led me to demand why I had such an affliction, and I saw my first unmistakable though brief vision of the woman handing the flask with poison to the man who came to her door.

My sense of guilt and disconnect from Light and Source after my misdeed in Atlanta quite likely played some role in my heart attack on learning of the death of the Prophet Yeshua in Judea in my life as Mariam. Awareness of loss of connection, even distant connection, was just too painful to bear. There was likely an element of self-punishment in my being burned at the stake as a heretic because I could not renounce a man I loved and knew was good. That led to spiritual confusion. I was guided through that confusion by the bishop who was my guide in the early decades of this lifetime, but I had very conflicted feelings toward him. The loving beings who serve the Light are always trying to help us work through conflicted emotions and get back on track, but they never force us in any way so we may wander in our confusion through many lifetimes. That confusion can influence the belief systems we adopt. Perhaps I would have taken a lot more positive tack through my imprisonment after the Austrian peasant revolt failed if I had a better developed spiritual side, but as a participant in the "Enlightenment" I had decided spirituality was a superstition that kept people submissive.

In lifetimes where I have been involved with shamanic principles or practices including communication with spirits I have also been impacted by that decision in Atlantis to try to gain energy, light and status –glory, actually- through wrong means. The terrors and confusion I experienced as the young woman medium in Crete were a painful result of feeling disconnected from the Light, especially the fear of having my essence, my being, captured by forces or beings of darkness. Of course I was subject to the power of suggestion by those who exploited me, but I was vulnerable to that power of suggestion precisely because it resonated deeply with my inmost fears. Those fears also led me to encountering Hohn the Nordic shaman which was frightening, especially learning that he did in fact acquire some kinds of energy by triggering the deaths of strangers in his territory, and he himself fell victim to a similar practice by a shaman of greater force. My realization that Black Mama killed the slave owner through the influence and temporary possession by angry, vengeful spirits of parents was also very disconcerting. My fear of the Black Bird was another echo of that fear, as was my fear of Mara and also of whatever other more powerfully negative entity I sensed behind her.

I am humbly grateful to report that I have had almost complete healing of my terrors of dark forces through my profound experience as the "bat out of hell" (self-created hell) reunited with Jesus and finally able to accept his forgiveness and forgive myself. I say humbly because we should always be wary that dark forces exist and would like to steal or absorb our light by deceiving us, so pride truly deserves its reputation as a pitfall, but we can also extend our moment to moment awareness of the Light and the readiness of allies in Light to help us if we ask for their help with right intention (ie, in mutual service to the Light, not self aggrandizement).

The Polynesian shaman did not seem disturbed by his attempt to shelter the spirits of dying children nor have any fear of dark spirits or forces himself. Either that was a lifetime before that fateful decision in Atlantis, perhaps in Lemurian times or at an earlier Atlantean time than the life of the herbalist, or his was a lifetime where I was helped to shield out the influence of my bad decision because there was other more important work to do and lessons to learn in that lifetime.

ASSISTANTS

There are many forms of help available for those who want to explore their past lives. Your own meditative reflections and dreams may open doors. Regression therapists, hypnotherapists who have experience doing past life regressions, past life readers, past life specialty astrologers, and some body workers may be fruitful channels. There are also taped regression instructions that some people find useful. If you are comfortable working with beings not in bodies, you may find assistance from angels, personal guides or special mission guides. Support groups for the purpose of common exploration can be very helpful. You might want to seek a study group of the Association for Research and Enlightenment (Edgar Cayce study group) in your area. Pay attention to what resonates with you. If you are mainly just interested in clearing your own aura and resolving your own issues you will find your intuition guides you to that end. If it is important to you to try to verify historical information that emerges for you, then set that intention clearly and your intuition will likely guide you to library, online and/or family historical records that can sometimes provide you external verification. Some people also use applied kinesiology (muscle testing) to gain internal validation for distinguishing what is true from what is misunderstanding or distortion.

If you feel called to explore your past lives, it is likely that elements of past lives appear in your dreams already, and will certainly do so if you ask your dreams to open that channel for you. If you don't already do so, it is very useful to keep a dream journal and have some notation system for any image or element or feeling you have any hunch might be related to a past life. Have a notation system for any recurring or similar images because these allow you to learn your own dream vocabulary. Images can have universal symbolic or archetypal meanings but more often than not the meaning is specific to the context in which the dreamer first saw or heard of and made association to that image. As you keep a dream journal and reflect on each night's dreams, recurring images or themes become a way your unconscious communicates with you in your personal language that you come to understand. When you develop that level of rapport with your unconscious you can begin to ask for it to answer your questions through dreams or through imagery that arises in receptive meditative states where you are not focused on any specific meditative exercise. You can gain important memory fragments this way, and this also "primes the pump" so that work done with a regression therapist is even more productive.

Sometimes past life elements – feelings, images or body sensations or symptoms – arise spontaneously in body work so you might want to check that your body worker knows what to do with that experience. Some body workers also see or intuit past life impressions and may share these. A body worker with good boundaries will ask if you want to be told such impressions, since they can generate emotional reactions because you are in a vulnerable receptive state. Also, there is no guarantee that what comes into the awareness of the body worker is truly your past life material and not his/her own.

Past Life Readings

A meaningful past life reading depends largely on the psychic skill of the reader but also on the openness of the person getting a reading. We can hide a lot of information from ourselves and others, both consciously and unconsciously, which affects what a reader can pick up. The reader may get accurate snatches or more symbolic, archetypal stories or glimpses. Of course, an overlay of the reader's own psyche and issues is always a factor, to a greater or lesser degree. You can ask the reader to report only what s/he sees and not embellish any story. This can help relieve the reader of any pressure to perform (that almost always leads to distortions) and relieve you of unrealistic expectations so you are more genuinely open to whatever emerges. You may seem to get less this way but what you get is more likely to be on target.

REGRESSION THERAPIES

Regression therapies vary in levels of direct experience of the person regressed. This ranges from getting a psychic reading of a past life to dream recall to hypnotic trance induced viewing to altered state partial recall to full body re-experiencing (levels of re-enactment) to spontaneous flashback. Each of these has potential benefits and downsides. It is best for the individual seeking regression and the regression practitioner to look together at what method in the practitioner's skill set would best fit the particular person and issue s/he wants to work with.

Preparation for any regression work is frequently a significant factor impacting effectiveness.

How do you prepare? Any practice you do that helps you uncover and release emotional energy is valuable. Journaling, mindfulness meditation and chakra clearing meditations, bio-energetic and sensorimotor release exercises have proven useful. Particularly beneficial is a practice of being aware of your feelings and allowing them space, not needing to push them away or eat or shop or get busy or drink, and experiencing them resolve and dissipate as you give them space without getting caught up in whatever story or event has generated them. This takes practice and you will find some days you feel more able to do this than others. If you haven't done this before, start with small irritations (ex., someone cutting you off in traffic) and work your way up to larger issues with stronger feelings that are more challenging to release. Allow tears, shaking with fear, and the heat of anger that wants sound or movement. Arrange to do this in a safe place, and allow sound or large muscle movement. Try to stay aware of the sensations of the emotion in your body much more than the thought that generates the emotion and you will find that the emotional energy dissipates. This is worth the practice it takes because you will improve mental and physical health this way, hopefully avoiding any permanent residue from current dramas in your life as well as opening the doors to release energies from unresolved past life issues.

How you process the information from a past life reading or regression also makes a difference. If the reading has not been recorded, try to write it down as accurately as you can as soon as possible, before you reflect on it or try to process it. Processing will naturally tend to shift the story – that is part of the value of processing, to evolve the way you experience the story. As you begin to release fear, anger, grief, worry or other emotions you eventually begin to see or intuit more of the story, including the feelings and motivations of other people in the story, which you may have subliminally known but not been conscious of, due to flooding by your own emotions. You can return to a recording of the story (oral or written) to gauge how much charge has dissipated or still needs release, and how well you have integrated that experience into your history and your sense of yourself. Integrating our experiences leads to feeling calmer, stronger, more whole, more connected to our essence and more able to face whatever circumstances come our way. We gradually build our realization and conviction that some essential core of us does survive bodily death and circumstances, and also that tensions, dramas and conflicts will fade away when energy is released from them.

If you want the help of a regression therapist, check with IBRT.org – International Board of Regression Therapists – for a recommendation in your area. They have a screening program and requirements that clinical therapists must meet. The Light Institute in Galileo, New Mexico offers a 4-7 day series of past life regression therapy sessions. The Association for Research and Enlightenment can also recommend therapists. It is very helpful to feel a good intuitive connection with a regression therapist because your unconscious will have to trust that person in order to come forward for you. Sometimes you may feel there are past life indicators and you are comfortable with your therapist but nothing much comes up in past life regression sessions. This is usually an indicator that your unconscious knows it is better to keep the amnesia barrier in place for the time being. It may be that you need to work through more childhood or adult relationship issues from this lifetime first, or gain greater ease in emotional and/or physical release work before your psyche is ready to open doors. Sometimes group regression is very helpful for this. There is always the risk that you pick up on someone else's experience more than your own, especially if you are naturally empathic. If you stay with what comes up for you and sit quietly with it later you will usually get either a fading away if it wasn't really yours or a recurring sense of resonance if all or a significant portion of your experience is truly your own.

Group Regression

This normally occurs in a workshop or class where people are able to sit in very comfortable positions or lie on the floor. (Discomfort from sitting on hard or straight chairs or compression along the spine can interfere with the flow of energy through the body and inhibit memories, emotions, sensations, etc.) Most often a regressionist or hypnotherapist will induce a trance in all those who are open to participating. Occasionally groups might use pre-recorded guidance for this purpose. Imagery designed to open the door to memory banks is used and time given for inner experience and then the participants are called back to the present moment and encouraged to become fully present in their current body.

One advantage of the group method is that the group energy often heightens the individual experience, because there is more energy in the room available to work with, and tracking memories does take a kind of energy and focus, even in a very relaxed state. There is also the strength of group intention to reinforce individual desire. However, by the same token, group energy can interfere with individual experience because there is a tendency for minds and hearts to entrain — that is, for individuals to experience similar wavelengths and energy frequencies that lead to similar stories or themes. While this can make for rich stories and encouraging experience, it can also lead to elements of "group think" that override what would be individually more relevant. This is because the hypnotic trance state, whether it occurs spontaneously, as for example at a music concert or political rally, or is more deliberately induced, is a state that naturally supports telepathy. So it is common for characters or themes to repeat in variations of individual stories.

The person(s) with the most coherent heart and brain wave signals will generally spread their influence, though it is hard to determine ahead of time who that might be, since it usually has no correlation at all with the most talkative or dramatic person or dominant personality. Much also depends on how strong and how open are the energy boundaries of individuals, so if you find yourself in a group regression and want your experience to come from your own memory bank as much as possible, set a clear strong intention for this and visualize yourself sealed in an energy body with an impermeable membrane. Of course, you may lose out on the advantage of the group momentum this way but your experience will be more your own. Be sure to dissolve this sealed membrane after the event so you do not prevent yourself from taking in the beneficial energies you need to sustain your health on a regular basis.

It is best if post regression sharing in a group of what emerged is kept to summaries of place and themes rather than detailed accounts, to help each person dwell in and derive the most benefit from their own experience. There can be a natural temptation for the leader to want to demonstrate the benefit of the group regression through exciting accounts and for those who love to have an audience to recount their story in detail, but this is not really helpful for the majority of group participants, and is best shared at a later time. And of course you should never feel compelled to share, and your experience may be either raw or hazy and best left to ongoing inner processing.

This is also a recommended approach for assessing imagery, story lines and interpretations that come to you through past life readings and specialty or karmic astrology readings.

Individual Hypnotic Regression

This is usually done lying down on a couch or reclining in a chair designed to support deep relaxing. A hypnotist will usually give verbal instructions that encourage relaxing and guide the person toward inward experience of images and story bits that can float up from the subconscious when we are deeply relaxed but not quite asleep. This is somewhat analogous to dream imagery, except that when we are asleep we cannot report the imagery we see. There are states of dream sleep from deep to lighter. Our most coherent dreams, which may seem to be stories or fragments of stories, come to us in this light sleep state which is similar to hypnosis. This is a state in which a subject is more open to suggestion, and suggestions should be made in careful wording that evokes a story without suggesting any specific details. Avoiding leading questions or suggestions enhances the likelihood that whatever story elements emerge are authentically from the subject's memory bank, which is beyond time. It is very common for symbols and bits to appear that seem random and meaningless but in fact are often related either to the story theme or they are signals that the consciousness is connecting with a deeper layer of the psyche.

Hypnotic regression can vary in focus from the individual simply seeing or witnessing a story – often from a safe distance if there is any hint of trauma – to entering into the first hand experience of the past life person. Witnessing is generally more comfortable and can certainly provide useful information to reflect on and work with at a later time. Rarely does witnessing by itself bring about any real resolution of conflict or lasting relief or change of belief. But it can provide key information for resolving feelings through other modalities used later such as EMDR – Eye Movement Desensitization & Reprocessing, EFT – Emotional Field Therapy (aka tapping), clearing negative beliefs with specific journaling and affirmation exercises, etc.

Hypnotic regression can frequently (though not always) also give the hypnotist access to a realm of the subconscious where knowledge and wisdom are held, most often without any images, but rather a more direct intuitive knowing. Conversing with the "Inner Knower", "Inner Self Helper", "Inner Guide" or whatever term you prefer, can yield insight about whatever emerged in regression, how it might fit in with the subject's current life, why events happened, what potential lessons were meant or available to be learned, how the regression story may relate to other lifetimes, who in the current life time might be a reincarnation of someone from the past lifetime, etc. This kind of knowledge doesn't necessarily bring any change by itself, but it can provide the subject with very useful insights for reflection that can help bring success to further emotional healing processes.

Past Life Regression Re-Enactment

First we should be clear that regression re-enactment is not the same as staged historical re-enactments of scenes from the civil war, medieval times, or other historical period pieces, although the urge of the psyche to clear out tensions from past lives may inspire people to participate in historical re-enactments, and may prime the pump for them to remember details from a specific lifetime with the help of individual hypnotic regression. Many people have been able to gain sufficient detail to verify the historical accuracy of the past life personage who comes through them. Even this does not fully guarantee that the person undergoing regression was truly that historical person because it is possible for spontaneous mediumship to occur (see discussion of mediumship) but it is at least highly likely.

Past life regression re-enactment therapy depends on the skillset and preferred modes of the therapist as well as the openness of the client to levels of experience. The methods I use were honed in several week-long training sessions over 3 years with Roger Woolger, along with 20 guided practice sessions and various other regressions which qualified me to obtain clinical certification from the International Board of Regression Therapists. At various times Roger referred to his therapy modalities as regression therapy and/or matrix therapy, because deep seated core issues very often showed up as repeating past life stories as well as in utero incidents and/or early childhood incidents in this lifetime. It seems the psyche seeks to be whole and repeatedly re-creates circumstances and scenarios around core issues that we have not resolved.

A typical session would find the client lying comfortably on a thick mat or mattress on the floor, so the body can shift easily from deep relaxation or stillness to unimpeded movement. The therapist sits on a cushion nearby, although some therapists find this too uncomfortable for sustained work and elect to sit on a chair next to a wide couch for the client. Preparation for the session begins with defining what the client would like to resolve: a recurring body ailment or accident tendency, a chronic feeling, a belief that doesn't seem to have come from parents or known source in this life, a recurring relationship pattern, or an obsession/fascination with some historical period, geographic place or setting that has déjà vu elements, such as seeing themselves in a temple they have never seen in this lifetime. A recurring dream is also a good starting point. We start with guiding the client to feel grounded and present in their current body, since the body is an excellent gateway into its own history stored in its energy field (aura). A body sensation or location of an ailment, a strong emotional feeling that has a correlate in the body, or a feeling of familiarity with a place or key detail in a recurring dream– can all be examples of starting points into a story.

A typical session unfolds in the following way.

Therapist suggestion: "Let yourself be fully in your body and breathe deeply, fully in and out a few times…"

"Now tune in to (selected gateway/entry point….an area of the body, a strong emotion, a dream fragment, a person or pattern there are recurring issues with, etc.…)

"Focus intently on that……."

"More and more tuned in to ……."

When the therapist sees the client show some sign of being clearly connected with the gateway point, "Find yourself in another time and place and body which is very connected with …(entry point)."

"What are you aware of….?"

"Feel the body you are in……look down at your feet……what do you see?" (May prompt by asking "Are you barefoot or do you have shoes on? What kind of shoes? Are they the feet of a grown up or a child or….?"

"Are you a man/boy or a woman/girl?"

A Labyrinth of Lifetimes

"How old are you?"

"What are you wearing…?" If the past life person seems unsure, "Look down at your clothes or feel them….." With experiential therapy it is very important to get a clear sense of the body one is in along with the surrounding circumstances, which help anchor the person in that lifetime. The story will be relived through what the past life personality sees, hears, touches, smells, tastes….and these pathways help with memory recall of other people, events, reactions and actions of the past life person.

From there the story unfolds with minimal interruption from the therapist because the goal is to follow the cord of memory. If there seems to be an overabundance of trivial detail the therapist may say "Move forward to an important event…… what happens now….?"

At significant points the therapist may also ask the past life person "What do you feel about that?"

Or, the therapist may ask questions that deepen the focus or clarify a discrepancy, although usually the story unfolds in a flow of its own. Even experienced therapists marvel at how a story unfolds from itself, often with surprising twists the therapist would not have guessed. The story takes on a life of its own, and a therapist who asks a leading question or makes a suggestion when a story is unfolding in this way can be quite surprised to hear an emphatic contrary insistence from the past life personality. This is generally true even when the story could fit into common categories such as Mission not accomplished, Sudden permanent separation from a loved one, Betrayal, Victim, Surprise attack, Imprisonment, etc.

When the key events or experiences have emerged the therapist suggests the past life person move forward to check for anything else significant and past that to the time and circumstances of their death. Special attention is paid to feelings and thoughts at the time of death because these are often carried forward as belief complexes that shape future life experiences. The person is encouraged to move through the death consciously, because this helps build realization of continuity of consciousness – ie, that our consciousness survives death and emerges again in other lifetimes. If the death is traumatic the suggestion is given that the person has the option of pulling out of the body to watch rather than experience, but still asked to record the final thoughts and feelings from that lifetime.

Since the purpose of experiential regression is therapeutic, ie, the release of residual tensions and the resolution of conflicts and/or frustrated yearnings, there is much work left to do.

The Bardo is a term given by Tibetans to various stages between lives. In past life therapy we use the term to refer to a state of open connection to inner wisdom that generally is available right after a regression experience has emerged.

I have learned to ask the person what they do after they die, to discern whether they realize their body is dead. One of the first regressions I guided for an anorexic young woman plagued with suicidal thoughts. In her past life she was an Indian brave in his prime who got a surprise tomahawk to the neck from an enemy Indian. He was determined not to die and focused such intense concentration and will in his throat that even though he died, in his subsequent life he had terrible thyroid problems and bloated up to 450 pounds. That poor fellow did commit suicide due to the shaming remarks inflicted on him for his condition. Some people experience light after they die. If this is universal, not everyone remembers it. Some experience themselves wandering, a little lost, and perhaps begin to move into another related lifetime. The complexities of these lives each needed attention to unravel. I usually tell the client the second story is for another day and ask them instead to look for or ask for a guide, since we all typically have guides available to help us cross over.

I then ask, "What is important to learn from this lifetime of……..(character just lived)?"

This can lead into a fruitful discussion of purpose and meaning. It can also be an occasion to encounter other persons from that lifetime, for instance children whose death caused anguish to their parents, lost lovers or mentors, etc. Knowing we are reunited can help relieve grief. The Bardo is also a place where victims can encounter their abusers and tell them whatever they want to or wished they could have said. Some experience their abusers being willing to listen and repent; others seem deaf but a guide can assure the past life person that their abuser will see the light eventually and regret their wrongdoing. Individual stories will suggest other possibilities.

Another phase of therapeutic work is to return to key points in the story to give vent to feelings. This can be done before or after the Bardo processes, depending on where the energies seem most inclined to go in each individual case. Catharsis seems to clear the way for especially deep intuitive Bardo work. The therapist will have noted points in the past life story where there seems to be significant energy in a feeling (which may only be shown through body tension, so the therapist should be a keen, experienced observer). The therapist will direct the client to re-enter the story at each of those points (which are still fresh in mind) and encourage tears, large muscle anger release by pounding a pillow or screaming fear or rage into it. Shaking can be a good release for fear. At the very least, the past life person is assured it is now safe to feel and give space and attention to feelings, and imagine how they might like to express them. The therapist will encourage the person to speak dilemmas clearly. It is also important to tune into the body to notice any places where tensions or residues of feelings may still be lodged. Sometimes conscious release is enough at that point, but often further body work may be needed. Where there is tension from an action the past life person was not able to complete, for example, delivering a battle blow, climbing to the top of a place where that was cut off by a sudden fall, reaching out to grab someone or something, running with a purpose to get somewhere or dozens of other possibilities, it can be useful for the person to stand up and consciously complete that motion, one or more times until the energy feels spent. This can be especially useful if a person has been victimized and in their rage wanted to turn on their abuser but they wouldn't or couldn't for whatever reason and felt powerless. Cardboard centers of paper towels or wrapping paper make good "swords" for this and bath towels make good padding for the therapist.

One other useful topic to explore in the Bardo is the roles that people from the past life may now play in the current life, often with some repetition of the dynamics at play in their past life relationships, or a mirroring of those or a role reversal. A guide can still be called in if needed for confirmation, although often the client feels sure of that past life character's current role in the client's life, in which case s/he does not need this added support. Their intuition has been cleared enough for that recognition and should be more available to help them in the future with that person.

One other aspect of experiential regression that should always be attended to and proves central in some cases is what happens to the body after death. If the body is treated respectfully according to the cultural customs of the time and place that may be enough to know. But in case of catastrophes, it may help to find the body or collect the remains and give them an imaginal funeral. It is best to ask the past life person what they would like done with their body. Perhaps chosen animals come and bury it and the body thus returns to mother earth. Especially where the person has been denied usual respectful burial for some political or religious reason, appropriate blessings and rituals can be observed in the Bardo. Recall the story of Luc who very much wanted "the prayers" said over him and feared he was unworthy of heaven without them. Remember that we are not trying to play God or St. Peter or judge so much as attending to the person's FEARS, RESENTMENTS or BELIEFS. Black Mama also needed an honorable funeral experience appropriate for her after the degradation and shame of hanging naked.

A regression that includes all these levels of therapeutic work generally requires about two hours. If a client doesn't have the stamina to do this in one session, the completion work can be done in a later session, preferable later the same day or the next day.

Spontaneous Past Life Regression

Particularly after a person has been through several detailed past life regressions, they may find themselves very drawn to a particular time or place, or feel intuitively that an issue has strong roots in a past life. They may be able to find a quiet space with two hours of uninterrupted solitude in which to delve into a past life using whichever entry gate – geographic sense, strong emotion, physical sensation or ailment, recurring pattern, etc. has the strongest energy for them. It can be very challenging to sustain a regression without assistance. Previously taped instructions may be helpful here. It is valuable to attend to whatever feelings or dilemmas arise in the regression, to work with them as much as possible, through journaling, maybe using mime or dance to express an emotion or perhaps using art – for example, painting, clay modeling or simple sketching – as a follow up way to express the feelings and insights from the regression.

Resonance

How do you evaluate the information that arises from a reading or a past life regression? Clients often mention how "true" or "real" an experience has felt, especially with experiential regression. The information or feelings that emerge ring true or resonate with them. In a fully therapeutic past life regression, you will have been urged to focus on what comes up until as complete a story as possible has emerged and been recorded in some way. Then you would be encouraged to return to the dominant energy or feelings from the story and allow them space and expression. Very often clients experience strong feelings and such a sense of how real the story feels that the truth of it is self-evident to them. If their belief system does not support reincarnation they can come to doubt their experience with the passage of time, but this is evidence of common amnesia that can happen to blot out any trauma or evidence that does not match our beliefs. A study was done on women who were treated for rape at a trauma center. Nine months later more than one third of them "forgot" or even denied that they had ever been there. After two years the number was over forty per cent. Clients are much more likely to integrate their regression experience if they do the therapeutic processes listed above, and much more likely to benefit from lasting ease or at least ongoing significant reduction in physical and emotional tensions and conflicts from issues that have manifested in the regression. Synchronicity often arises in the form of finally finding just the right body worker or herbal remedy that brings relief from chronic physical symptoms after a successful regression – because the subconscious belief system is no longer blocking it. All of these are ways that may fuel direct or indirect resonance with a regression – that is, an inner knowing of the truth and actuality of the regression, whether or not every detail proves historically accurate if it is investigated.

IMPORTANCE OF INTENTION

Past Life Regression is most effective when both the regressionist and the client have clear intention. Is the goal…

1. To find some interesting history?
2. To learn more about an era?
3. To learn one's previous incarnational history?
4. To relieve a bodily symptom or condition?
5. To shift a chronic emotion (ex fear, anger, grief, guilt)?
6. To change a pattern of relationship dynamics, for ex. Repetition of abandonment?
7. To know more about one's unconscious beliefs or the roots of conscious beliefs?
8. To explore any prior relationship with a person in the client's current life?
9. To clear one's aura or promote soul development?
10. To learn through experience what regression can feel like, in order to become a regressionist?
11. To bring forward a past talent or gift that could benefit the client or others in this lifetime?

The above are all goals that motivate people to seek past life regression. If the goal is simply to discover information that can be checked against historical records, the regressionist might effectively give very specific suggestions within a hypnotic trance.

However if the goal is to relieve a symptom pattern – a physical ailment, chronic emotion or fixed belief that the client would like to change or a repeating pattern, it is best to respect the psyche by not telling the psyche to "find the past life root of this problem" because the root of the problem might not be in a past life of client. It might be in a forgotten childhood event or a conversation overheard in utero. The client could have an unconscious motive that the symptom or belief or pattern is still serving. Or the source might be ancestral influence or intrusion by an entity. Since neither the client nor the regressionist has a crystal ball and regression is not a psychic reading, it is best to give suggestions that invite the psyche to reveal the true source or cause for a symptom, and later the conditions (ex. new thoughts, bardo encounters, body work, entity release) needed to replace the symptom with a healthy pattern. From there I find it very useful to let the psyche lead and I follow its indications. This is partly an intuitive art, partly the result of good training, and partly the fruit of experience.

If the goal is to explore one's incarnational history or clear one's aura, the client can be directed to find a lifetime that has an important influence on this lifetime. One option is to set a target of finding a life where the client used a talent or skill that could be brought forward. The search can also be for a desired attribute. For example, I was searching for confidence and an experience of abundance to replace anxiety when "Enuf" came through, and recalling/reliving that experience has served me well on several occasions and continues to teach me.

In general, past life regression tends to be more successful when there is strong motivational energy – either a desire for relief or fascination with a period of history or a geographical place or the process of incarnation itself, along with soul development. If a regressionist is using straight hypnosis, and a client with only idle curiosity turns out to be a good hypnotic subject, then interesting results can also come through, but in general the psyche shields us from our memories, even positive ones, with an amnesiac barrier that we need sufficient energy to pass through. The combined intentionality of client and regressionist can very often provide sufficient momentum to pass that barrier. On the rare occasion that nothing arises, I have learned to respect the psyche's wisdom. My usual hunch in that case is that the client would not be able to successfully integrate the knowledge or energy or emotions that would pour out if the doors to memory were opened. I therefore ask the client to reflect on safety – in images, and in general in life. When there is enough sense of security, the doors will usually open, but that might not happen on the day you first ask about it; that security might need time to develop.

If there is an intruding ancestor or entity, s/he may have a very different intention that hinders regression. Sometimes their agenda includes blocking the client from awareness of their presence and influence. More discussion of this will follow in "Entity Involvement".

Comparison of Past Life Regression Therapy Approaches

Which form of past life regression is best? That depends on your intention. If your intention is simple curiosity and you want to learn about possible other lifetimes, any of these methods can give you images to reflect on which may be more or less true.

If your goal is to relieve symptoms and/or clear your aura and transform yourself, you have the greatest opportunity for achieving that if you enter into the past life experience. That is due to state-dependent learning. When you are actually IN a situation is when your body records a reaction to it that gives rise to a mental perception that triggers an emotional response. That body sensation/thought/feeling will either confirm existing beliefs or stand in contrast to them, creating conflict. Simply thinking about a desired belief or repeating affirmations is not usually enough to dislodge an impression that has been formed at a body/mind/feeling level. To change a belief formed physically, mentally and emotionally is most likely to succeed if you return to the circumstances in which it was formed, at least return energetically. If a client is among the 15–20% of people who are excellent hypnotic subjects and the hypnotherapist is sufficiently skilled and trained in the nuances of psychological functioning (ie, an experienced psychotherapist with extensive experience working with the unconscious and semi-conscious) this can sometimes be achieved through hypnosis. If one of those skillsets is lacking, there is more likelihood of changing the sensation/thought/feeling complex by re-experiencing the circumstances with the addition of the larger knowing (ie, by today's personality) that this is after all a past life regression, not a current drama, and there are new possible ways to see the event. Especially in the altered state that arises naturally with the catharsis (release) of emotion, the client has more access to brain plasticity – ie, the capacity to change habitual neuron formations that have been inherited from past beliefs.

The new neurons branches that begin to form get a boost from that energy, but they must still be reinforced through the use of affirmations, preferably with the addition of emotional energy (ie, practice feeling the new feeling that goes with the new belief). As we have seen from some of the regressions above (Austrian peasant revolt leader, Atlantean herbalist forgiven, Black Mammy, Hohn, and others), considerable additional work in other modalities such as body work and energy work may be needed to gain maximum transformational benefit from a past life regression.

DISCERNMENT OF DARK AND BRIGHT SHADOW

The majority of past life regressions proceed as simple past lives. Some issues seem to evoke two lifetimes of almost equal energy. Sometimes what emerges is a life story so far removed from our historical perspective that it seems to come from another realm altogether, much like a lucid dream. This is connecting to a realm of the unconscious that could be past life but might be symbolic, or archetypal, or might in fact be a portal to another dimension. Other stories emerge in such halting, guarded ways that the experienced regressionist begins to sense there is more than one consciousness involved in the story. The added element might be an ancestor or some other entity influencing the client. Here we will explore a range of possibilities. It is always important that the regression therapist remain calm and grounded and assure that the client is safe and has a manageable level of any emotional discomfort that may arise. It is incumbent on the therapist to get enough training to assure these conditions. Remember that it is always possible to suggest that the client change perspective and view any images from a safe distance rather than directly experience their circumstances. And should the need arise there is always assistance available, from other elements in the psyche such as the Inner Guide or Inner Self Helper.

Kathy Bornino

Psychologist Carl Jung spoke extensively about dark shadow elements of our psyche – instinctual urges and emotions which we hide from conscious awareness, as well as bright shadow elements – gifts and talents which we have not developed and very often fear developing for various reasons.

Dark shadow elements include but are not limited to: aggressive and sexual urges, desire to possess and control, lust for glory or wealth, and our conflicts and guilt feelings around such urges. Anyone who undergoes a series of regressions will typically first encounter one or more lifetimes in which s/he fell victim to some other person, and later encounter a previous life in which s/he hurt or exploited someone else. This growing awareness is what underlies realization of the laws of karma. This range of experiences gives us the opportunity to explore unconscious or conscious but unexplained feelings of victimhood, abandonment, powerlessness, anger, revenge, aggression, desire, guilt, remorse, grief, fear and also compassion, understanding and forgiveness and the joys of reunion, love and giving. Since the feelings in previous lifetimes are often interwoven with feelings we experience in this lifetime, regression therapy gives us the opportunity to work through much of our dark shadow elements which we might continue to puzzle over if we stayed within the limits of traditional psychotherapy and dream work.

Bright shadow elements might first seem like something we would eagerly explore – who would not revel in beauty or power or talents? And why would we find them so terrifying? Jung claimed they generated even more fear in us than dark shadow elements.

We may fear the loss of control that comes with feeling taken over by an urge, whether it be a seemingly harmless urge such as music or art (read about Van Gogh's torments) or a more conflictual gift such as psychic ability. We all have some access to our collective unconscious so we know messengers (including writers) have been killed for delivering messages (ex. Pearl Buck's novels about imperial China reveal it was common practice to kill the messenger who delivered unwelcome news to the emperor, usually a message he was forced under pain of death to deliver, an example of a fateful Catch 22.) Cassandra and other prophets are scorned as outcasts or tormented for warning people of impending disasters which might be prevented if people would listen and respond effectively. Doctors and other healers have been killed for failing to produce miracle healings – or for facilitating healing, and then being construed as working with the devil. There may also be reasons stemming from family dynamics that inhibit a person from developing potential gifts. A son with artistic gifts and a strong aversion to killing but born into a military family where all sons are expected to serve honorable duty might risk being an outcast if he developed his natural gifts and tendencies. A similar dynamic has been true for homosexuality in many places and cultures, and love might then appear in dreams and fantasies as a very frightening bright shadow, an urge to be repressed at all costs, and often hidden from the dreamer's awareness. Very often a talent brings with it a fear of making a mistake, of misusing the talent in some way, because there is a memory of having done just that. When the memory is cleared – the recognition of past action, guilt and remorse experienced, understanding of what urges led to the mistake, wisdom and humility acquired and integrated – then the person may be ready to face their fear of experiencing or developing their talent. Quite often the person also needs to find and garner experiences that help them own and develop courage and confidence before they can move forward in developing a gift.

There is also a mystical element in some encounters with bright shadow, which can also be a reason why these encounters can be terrifying. Behind the bright shadow can be the luminous void, encounter with the divine or dimensions beyond the known, with potential loss of ego identity. Of course the flip side, which makes this a bright or golden shadow, is that many people experience a hunger for the divine, so encountering and integrating bright shadow elements can be an awesome as well as discomfiting experience.

The inverse is also true, namely that a person can fear being taken over by dark forces, or may fear that has already happened. Here especially it is important for the regression therapist to remain calm and grounded, think of client safety first, and call into awareness the presence or realization of the Essential Self, Higher Self, Inner Self Helper, Inner Guide or whatever conceptualization fits for the client.

Experiences of fears of dark forces can range from simple forgotten childhood fears of the bogeyman from impressions formed at a pre-rational stage of development all the way to obsession by or seeming possession by an intrusive entity who does want to control the client for their own agenda.

This brings us to a discussion of intrusive entities.

ENTITY INVOLVEMENT

We have already discussed the presence of vibrational recordings that may exist as thoughtforms in families and have a noticeable impact on more sensitive family members. One instance was the air force family in which the young woman had recurring nightmares that were probably some form of the experience of her WWII bomber pilot uncle who had died in a car crash shortly after the allied victory, and the family had not known whether to ascribe his death to suicide or accident. Some ancestral spirits or entities stay with a family in more directive ways, intervening with approval, disapproval or warnings. Of course in practice it can be hard to distinguish these from fantasies or beliefs about what the ancestor might say if alive (ex, "Uncle Harry would turn over in his grave if he saw that…..") But there are instances where departed family members contact sensitive living members to convey information they want known, that no one alive would have known about, for example the location of money, jewelry, an important letter, photo, book, tool or some heirloom. Or they direct a family member to the right place at the right time to prevent an unforeseeable accident or other harm to a family member. And there are entities who contact psychics to convey information about a crime. They want that information delivered to police detectives, especially if they were murdered or otherwise the victim of foul play. All of these are usually isolated episodes, rather than extended attachments. In other cases a deceased mother, father or grandparent may remain connected to a child throughout their growing years, advising them through thought transference, comforting them with loving energy when they go through hard times, trying to prevent or mitigate abandonment feelings and loneliness. Those attachments make sense, and if the departed spirit moves on at an appropriate time, do no harm.

If the regression therapist suspects the involvement of an entity, s/he can simply ask "is there more than one being involved here…?" Either a simple acknowledgement or silence can let her/him know s/he is on the right track, and follow up inquiry can elicit at least the generic identity of the entity as child or adult and how they connected with the host and what function the entity fulfills.

Other attachments can be well meaning but not so beneficial. Why do spirit attachments occur? Usually because there is some resonance between the living person and the attaching entity, some function that each finds fulfilled by the other. Lonely creative children often have imaginary playmates which may be more than imaginary. Again there may be no harm if the entity moves on in a timely manner as the child outgrows the need or desire for them. But why does the entity attach in the first place? Sometimes an entity does not fully depart this plane when they die. If they die with a strong emotion or desire, they may have only a brief (almost no) experience of the Universal Light, and their strong emotion or desire may bring them back quickly to the earth plane, perhaps searching for a companion if they were a lonely child while alive, or a mother if they died as a child feeling fearful, or a child if they were a mother who died in childbirth or lost her child in traumatic circumstances. Very often such an entity has little or no realization that s/he might be impeding the growth of the host person in this life, and willingly withdraws if that is pointed out to them and s/he is helped to connect with a guide that helps them move on to the next plane of consciousness for her/him. It is also best in that case to help the host person, usually the client, come to awareness of what function the attaching entity fulfilled for them – ie, what was the "hook" the person had available that magnetically attracted the entity. This is especially necessary if the attaching entity has become quite habituated and comfortable with the host person, and is reluctant to depart. When the host hook is no longer present or very weak it becomes much more in the natural flow, the usual order of things for the entity to become aware of a guide or guides and willing to move on with their assistance. How do you discern this hook? My mentor Roger Woolger used to say "You have to ask the right questions…" All but the darkest entities will generally answer truthfully. The attaching entity will very often have their own story which they are willing to tell, that describes their experience and their needs/desires and what they were attracted to in the host entity. When they understand there are other more appropriate ways to get their needs met in other dimensions, they let go. This is less true of "earthbound" entities who have low vibrational energy and get these low vibrational goals met by siphoning energy from the host person, for example in the case of alcoholic entities who attach to alcoholic hosts. Here the help of powerful guides (who are always available when sincerely requested) and fervent, repeated prayer is frequently necessary, and can be supported by the prayer energy of other family members and compassionate helpers. Listening to an entity tell its story is much like listening to a past life account, but may be less grounded in a physical body because they are more removed from their actual physical history. Less time and attention should be given to helping them integrate their experience, because that is the work of their guides, but both entity and host may need a conscious goodbye. And the host client can often benefit from a specific new thought pattern to practice, such as connection with a current living person, in order to overcome any residual force of habit.

In the case of an entity with negative energy who does not want to depart, stronger measures are often necessary. At this point it may be appropriate for the regression therapist to explain the situation to the host client and refer them to a healer more experienced at entity removal. This is a rare occurrence but it does happen. Indigenous cultures around the world have experienced this and will normally have among them a shaman with expertise in this area. If the host person has a cultural background, the shaman from that culture may be the best referral. Sometimes their methods are hard on the physical body, because they want the host to be an unwelcome or displeasing energy for the intrusive entity. But they are generally not psychologically traumatizing because they understand the negative impact of fear, judgment and guilt. If the person has a Christian background there are exorcists who specialize in spirit removal, but before making a referral to one of these it is wise to ascertain that the person functioning as exorcist is himself healthy and understands the importance of avoiding the negative impacts of fear, judgment, guilt and any kind of condemnation no matter what the outcome. A cunning entity can easily use those elements to further confuse, demoralize and weaken the resistance or determination of the host person, potentially leaving that person even weaker.

A nest of intrusive entities can also exist, in which the first entity contacted seems more benign, but is actually a front for a more determined, more possessive being. Such a being may be attracted simply to the availability of human energy, since dark beings need light and energy to continue their current state of existence. If firm commands to go are not effective, along with strengthening the host, then this is almost certainly a case for referral or at least expert assistance and in depth support. The regression therapist should be very wary lest he himself fall under the influence of the wily thought suggestions and astral desire pull or negative emotion infusion from the invading entity (ex, fear, with an uncanny provocation of the therapist's own deepest fears.) Dark entities are known to be very crafty and frequently hide their methods. In their darkness they may also choose to lie and use any manner of deception or false appearance they can devise, of course at karmic peril to themselves but they are often past the point of caring about that. But it should be remembered that every being begins as light and is light in their essence, and the being should be assured they can return to the path of light and receive assistance to do that, no matter what their current level of darkness. Powerful positive guides are needed to assist in this! But the therapist should be aware that a pretense of turning toward the light can just be a deception designed to lull awareness and generate the false impression that all is well. Fortunately these situations are very rare occurrences but any regression therapist should be aware of these possibilities, and should one occur, protect the safety of the client by remaining calm and grounded and take appropriate measures. It is best to know of a referral source ahead of any need for one, but at least to reassure the client that the therapist will find one if not currently familiar with one.

The regression "Mara" illustrates several points about entities that are valuable to understand in past life work.

First, it is the **particular specific thought/feeling complex that a person is focused on at the time of death or surrender of consciousness** that gets lodged somewhere (aura? Akashic records? the non-local space time of quantum physics?) and stays with the psyche to be worked through in a future life.

In this case, this Norwegian courier girl THOUGHT she had made a mistake in delivering a letter and that her mistake put all her contacts – including people she loved or cared about -in mortal danger along with herself, which was more terrifying than death itself. In this lifetime, after this regression, my job sometimes involves extensive paperwork which can be boring and/or annoying but no longer engenders any panic in me. Also, I had occasion to send a letter to a loved one that had severe negative repercussions I did not foresee, but I had no panic when I sent the letter. The AHA! of realizing that the fate of the Norwegian courier was quite separate from her delivering a letter had freed me from an unconscious trigger that had plagued me for as long as I could remember.

Also In this case, the Middle Eastern desert entity Mara THOUGHT she was evil because she, along with her family traveling group, took in the curse and believed it. Thus, when asked on the Ouija board to identify herself, she characterized herself as an evil spirit, which was certainly enough to frighten me. Fear can add to the emotional vulnerability that allows an entity to intrude, or to remain because the host believes herself powerless, even if neither the host nor the intrusive entity has any true evil intention.

Many if not most intrusive entities are not really evil, but rather confused wandering spirits who look for solace and connection. They don't belong inside our aura so their presence can rightfully feel disturbing and that disturbed feeling can easily engender fear which makes the visitor seem bad or evil. How can a person discern whether a feeling is truly a response to an intrusive entity or merely one's own fear, or even potentially a truly ill-intentioned other presence? Roger Woolger would say "You have to ask the right questions….." But finding the right questions to ask can truly be a learned art, arising out of experience and intuition.

Not all beings have extended stays in the light when they die. The Tibetans who are masters of altered states and have been studying the death phenomena for centuries if not millennia tell us that all beings experience light when they die but many are not able to hang onto that experience and are quickly drawn back toward earthly and/or dark realms of thought/feeling/energy complexes. They may become earthbound spirits or attach themselves to embodied beings who have a particular vulnerability that sets up an affinity with one or more spirits with a reciprocal need.

One example of an affinity between beings might be a woman who has lost a child and in her grief craves a child, who attracts the spirit of a child who died in some trauma that interfered with his/her smooth transition into the light. Many children are unencumbered by trauma in this current life and pass easily back into the light when they die, but that is not always true.

If they were particularly frightened or feeling lost at the moment of death that panic might block their awareness of the light and they might then seek the warmth of a woman whose mother instinct is active and longing for a child. As their longings are satisfied they may each be able to detach and release the other and continue in normal soul evolution, but in some cases may need the help of prayer or the awareness of a heart centered intuitive to help them become aware and reassure them so they each have courage to move on. We all have guides helping us, so more often than not this process happens naturally. For example, a guide might prompt a mother semi-consciously as the mother or child hears words spoken by a kindly person who doesn't even know that guides are prompting him/her to say what the mother or child most needs to hear.

Another example could be a soldier who died in battle in the midst of trying to attain a particular goal. He may stay attached to that battlefield for a long while trying to achieve what he had focused on with such determination. A sensitive person wandering onto that battlefield (which might be a farm or home back yard or city park now) might feel "attacked" by the intensity of the focused energy that is still there. The soldier may need to be recognized and assured that he has done all he needs to do to fulfill his mission and the battle is over and either all is well now or the situation has evolved and it is time for him to answer the call to move on. If the sensitive person has his own traumatic past life memory of feeling suddenly attacked and dying unable to process the sudden attack and ejection from the body, there may be a reciprocal hook between the battlefield soldier and the sensitive battlefield visitor. That scenario would likely present as a crisis feeling and find its way to resolution rather quickly. However if the sensitive person does not understand what has happened to him/herself, he/she may carry forward additional residues of fear from this encounter that make him/her even more vulnerable in the future to the feeling of being attacked, and that fear could act as a magnet to further encounters where someone is or seems to be attacking the sensitive.

In another example, more than one psychic has been able to see an alcoholic person hanging out in a bar with disembodied souls who had been alcoholic in life and are now hovering around the aura of the alcoholic. If the alcoholic drinks to blackout, one or more of those spirits still craving alcohol may enter into the aura of the alcoholic so that they can vicariously fulfill their alcohol cravings through that drinker who still has a body. This of course complicates the treatment of addiction for that living alcoholic who must learn to manage not only his/her own cravings but those of the obsessing entity as well. Or, the obsessing entity may be found out and persuaded to leave. Some will leave voluntarily once they realize they are causing harm, which is not their intention, and once they are helped to see there is another pathway for them that opens toward the light and the company of a loving guide. Even with those who are resistant, the use of calm, loving, confident, positive insistence that this will be best and most fulfilling for them generally works better than condemning or trying to scare them away, which can easily make the host more fearful and vulnerable. Of course, the therapist or person who takes on the task of sending the entity on its way should have resolved any of their own fears and have a deep authentic conviction of the power of light and love to direct the situation.

In the Gospels Jesus regularly "casts out demons" by simply telling them to depart, but it is clear he has no shadow of doubt, perhaps because he is often in prayer (connection to Source) and has spent considerable time in the desert resolving his own fears and other potential ego thoughts or "temptations". The therapist needs to have confidence that some version of Christ or Light energy will make effective the therapist's directions to an entity.

ARCHETYPAL ENERGY

Renowned psychologist Carl Jung developed the concept of an archetype as a pattern of behavior or role that had the universal element of occurring across many cultures and usually connoted beliefs, feelings and outlook that went with that role. Hero, warrior, maiden, mother, father, crone, sage, victim, child, lover, and policeman would be examples of archetypal roles that could be embodied in or fulfilled by individual persons. There is some overlap with the idea of a stereotype although archetypes are clearly not racial since they occur across all cultures. Sometimes a symbol can become so strong it takes on an aura of archetypal energy. For example, the swastika and the term Nazi have developed well beyond German borders and have come to indicate the promotion of forceful dominance by a group (often alt right) that consider themselves to be a superior elite and entitled to repress, abuse and even eliminate a minority. A breast could be an archetypal symbol of nurturing and the mother archetype, although in a different context a breast might be a symbol of an archetypal lover.

Some people's lives seem to be governed by archetypal energy – they become their role. One manifestation of this phenomenon is how difficult it can be for soldiers to return home from active duty, especially if they do not get the help of a well-administered reintegration program and support for their individual challenges. Much PTSD involves getting stuck in the archetypal soldier role, especially since the soldier's life and that of his/her mates often depended on fully taking on the role. The movie "The Irishman" illustrated how a combat hero got hardened to the horrors his role required and he never lost his capacity to kill but rather made extensive use of it when he returned to civilian life. Our society encourages and is filled with "good" workers who become workaholics, our name for the archetypal worker who becomes his work role and neglects other facets of his life.

The experience of becoming a bat out of hell was not a delusion or hallucination in the usual psychological sense. I never lost touch with reality, always knew who I was, where I was, who I was with, what I was doing. Rather it was a kind of shamanic or spontaneous deep trance experience, of entering into an archetypal energy so fully that I could really feel the long bones and the soft hair of my wings and the claws of my feet. I could feel myself fly across the room and land upside down clinging with my claw feet to the sleeve on the forearm of the Christ. That fulfilled such a deep need that I truly did not want to leave that experience and only and let go with my claws after several minutes and continued very still for many more minutes. Only my concern for my therapist assistant who was missing lunch at last persuaded me to move out of the deep trance, but not before the whole episode was indelibly imprinted in my memory. It stands among the most profound and certainly transformative experiences of my life.

It is important to allow a regression experience – or an archetypal experience -to be whatever it is and whatever it wants to become, to enable the depths of the unconscious to come into conscious awareness and heal. And equally important for the client to return afterward to a state of being fully grounded before traveling away from the site of the regression and the watchful awareness of the therapist.

EPILOGUE

I hope very much that some part of my story or professional information and reflections has been of assistance to you. If you have read all or part of this account, you are certainly drawn to the topic of past lives, and I encourage you to pursue that nudge from your Spirit/Higher Self or your Soul (Mental/Emotional Body). There is certainly much for you to gain and you will be doing both yourself and humanity a tremendous service. When asked if he thought humanity could avert World War III, psychologist Carl Jung replied, "If enough people do their inner work". Clearing your aura of past life complexes that hinder you is the largest part of that work. I applaud any efforts you make in that direction. Bon Courage!!!

Resources

https://ibrt.org International Board of Regression Therapy

https://www.edgarcayce.org

You can also contact me at kathybornino@gmail.com for questions or assistance